The BiG Honkin' Activity Book

Kelly Gunzenhauser & Susan McBride

LARK BOOKS
A Division of Sterling Publishing Co., Inc.
New York / London

Editor
Joe Rhatigan

Art Director
Celia Naranjo

Illustrator
Susan McBride

Library of Congress Cataloging-in-Publication Data

Gunzenhauser, Kelly.
 The big honkin' activity book / Kelly Gunzenhauser & Susan McBride ;
illustrator , Susan McBride. -- 1st ed.
     p. cm.
 Includes index.
 ISBN 978-1-60059-349-9 (pb-pbk. with flaps : alk. paper)
 1. Amusements. 2. Games. 3. Creative activities and seat work. I.
McBride, Susan (Susan A.), 1962- II. Title.
 GV1203.G79 2009
 793.7--dc22

10 9 8 7 6 5 4 3 2 1

First Edition

Published by Lark Books, A Division of
Sterling Publishing Co., Inc.
387 Park Avenue South, New York, NY 10016

Text © 2009, Lark Books
Illustrations © 2009, Susan McBride

Distributed in Canada by Sterling Publishing,
c/o Canadian Manda Group, 165 Dufferin Street
Toronto, Ontario, Canada M6K 3H6

Distributed in the United Kingdom by GMC Distribution Services,
Castle Place, 166 High Street, Lewes, East Sussex, England BN7 1XU

Distributed in Australia by Capricorn Link (Australia) Pty Ltd.,
P.O. Box 704, Windsor, NSW 2756 Australia

If you have questions or comments about this book, please contact:
Lark Books
67 Broadway
Asheville, NC 28801
828-253-0467

Manufactured in China

ISBN 13: 978-1-60059-349-9

For information about custom editions, special sales, and premium and corporate purchases, please
contact Sterling Special Sales Department at 800-805-5489 or specialsales@sterlingpub.com.

For Bella, who is BIG;
and Murph, who likes to HONK;
and Peep, who is so ACTIVE;
and Star—please, stop eating my BOOKs.
—SM

This book is dedicated to Super Casey
to the Rescue, and to Reid, who
likes a good game of hat-ball.
—KG

Introducing... This Book!

The point of any good introduction is to um...introduce you to the book you're about to explore. It's our experience that in a book like this, most people don't read the introduction. (How long have you had this book before you read this paragraph?) So, we're not going to bog you down with a wordy introduction. You can bog yourself down with your own! Yes, we're asking you to do our job for us. Before you start, we have some things that HAVE to be here or our publisher will get mad, so don't forget to mention these points:

-- This book is big.

-- There are about 200 or so crazy, inventive, awesomely fun things to do including puzzles, quizzes, games, doodles, activities, and more.

-- The authors are extremely cool and talented.

-- Everything in this book can be done with a pencil, pen, some markers, and a few household junk-drawer items.

-- Great for the dentist's waiting room, car trips, tedious family reunions...whenever.

-- Can use it with friends, family, or by yourself.

-- Includes lots of blank pages in the back for extra fun.

-- You will NEVER be bored as long as you have this book with you.

Now remember, we're counting on you, so don't mess up.

Psychedelic Pachyderms

Every spring in the beautiful city of Jaipur, in northern India, all eyes are on the elephants. The people of Jaipur mark the beginning of spring by drawing, painting, and decorating their elephants. These vivid, bespangled giants are then paraded around the city, and the most beautiful beast is awarded a prize.

Perhaps you should adorn your elephants. If you don't have any, use the ones on the following pages.

Take Nine

Look at the first box. It has a nine-letter name for an animal in it. Yeah, really, it does. Look at the clue for each section and the starting letter. Then, draw a line from the starting letter to connect the rest of the letters in the word, in order. The letter has to touch the previous letter at a side or a corner. Answers are on page 246.

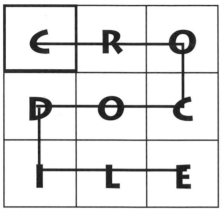

C	R	O
D	O	C
I	L	E

Toothy lizard.

E	M	R
R	A	O
T	H	W

Eat dirt!

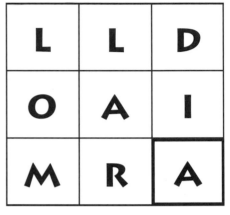

L	L	D
O	A	I
M	R	A

Has armor.

Y	F	R
L	U	E
B	T	T

Drinks out of (butter)cups.

A	C	K
B	L	B
D	R	I

Inky feathered friend.

A	G	O
L	R	N
Y	F	D

Fire-breathing insect?

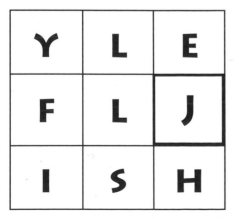

Y	L	E
F	L	J
I	S	H

NOT on a peanut butter sandwich.

C	D	E
E	E	T
P	I	N

Needs a hundred shoes.

P	U	C
I	R	P
N	E	O

Don't touch this guy!

10

Okay, now try to figure out these food-related puzzles without the starting letter box highlighted!

P	L	E
P	P	I
A	E	N

Hawaiian treat.

G	E	R
R	A	H
U	B	M

Meat and bread.

O	H	O
L	C	C
A	T	E

Favorite chip.

S	P	I
A	G	T
H	E	T

Long, skinny food.

P	C	H
I	A	I
S	T	O

This nut makes green ice cream.

P	A	R
S	S	A
U	G	A

This food grows in spears.

Make some of your own. Let your friends work on them.

Shuffle Off to...Your Kitchen Table

Here's one of the few games where it's fun for the players to knock each other out. Shuffleboard dates back to the Middle Ages and the days of King Henry VIII, when it was known as "shovillaborde." It started out as a game played on a table, but now there's also a version that's played on a smooth court—like the deck of a cruise ship. This is our own version.

1. Cut out the shuffleboard on the next page. Find another player and six checkers (three red and three black) or six plastic bottlecaps, or some other flat, round objects to be the disks. Each player gets three, so make sure you can tell them apart. Tape the shuffleboard to a tabletop, at least two feet from the edges of the table. Make sure you smoothly cover all of the edges with tape so that the disks can't slide under it.

2. Choose a player to go first. That player puts one disk on the edge of the table and flicks it with her finger—trying to get it to stop inside the triangle. The second player does the same thing with his disk. He gets the same chance to score, but if his disk knocks the first player's out of the triangle, then the first player doesn't get any points. So, the second player should try to knock the other player's disk out as well as score. Keep taking turns until you run out of disks,

3. Add up your points. If a disk lands in the 10 Off section, that player loses 10 points. And, if a disk is on two different sections, count the higher score. After you figure out your score for the first round, pick up your disks and play again. The second player goes first this time. Add the points from this turn to the points from the first turn, and keep taking turns. The first player to reach 50 points wins the game.

You can also play this game outside. Use chalk to draw the board on a driveway or sidewalk. Instead of checkers, use Frisbees, and push them with brooms.

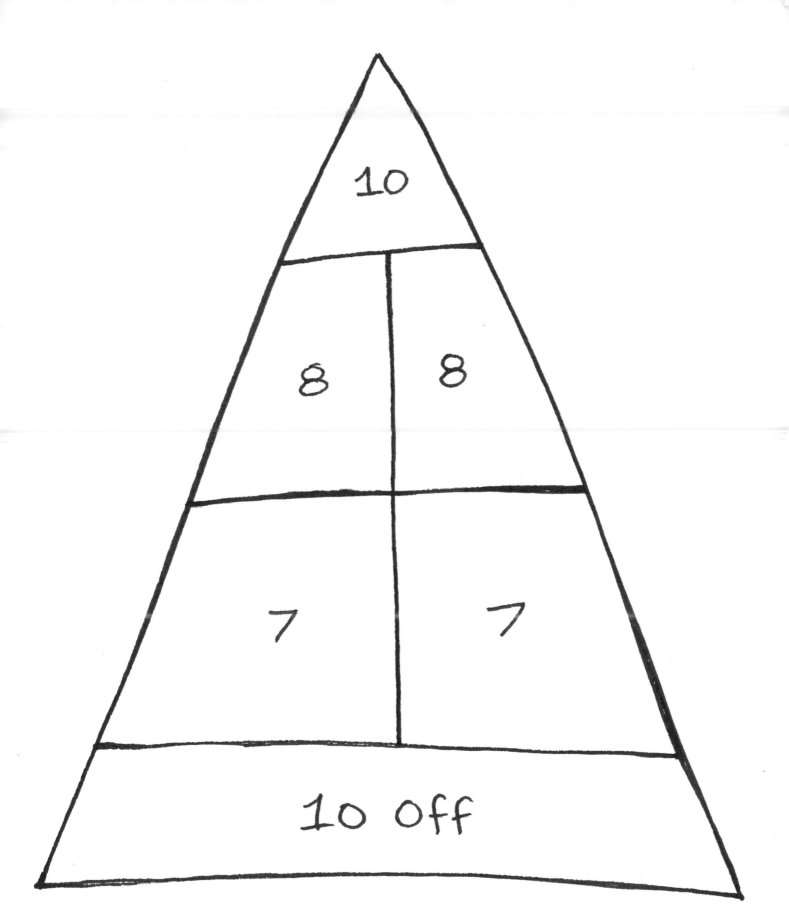

Page left blank on purpose.
Draw on it if you're not going
to play Shuffleboard. But, you
should really try it. It's fun.

Name Game

What's in a name? Plenty. When new parents name babies, they think about things like what names mean, what the initials will spell, and how popular the name is. Is your name common or unusual? What about your friends' names? Write down the names of everyone you can think of in five minutes. Use friends, teachers, classmates...anyone you know! When time's up, turn the page to see a list of the top 100 names for boys and girls. The top 10 names are worth 1 point each, the next 10 are worth 2 points, and so-on. (They're listed in alphabetical order so you can find them easily.) Add up the points and see how you score. If you come up with any names that aren't on the list, give yourself 11 points for each one.

Score:
56-186: Your friends and family have popular names.

187-373: Some of your friends' parents got a little creative.

374-560: Wow, awesome! What planet are you living on, anyway?!

What shall we name the baby, honey?

He sounds like an Owen, or a Nicholas... maybe a Nathaniel?

BOYS' NAMES

Aaron-6	Jackson-4
Adam-7	Jacob-1
Adrian-7	Jaden-9
Aidan-5	James-2
Aiden-3	Jason-6
Alejandro-10	Jayden-5
Alex-7	Jeremiah-8
Alexander-2	Jesús-8
Andrew-1	John-2
Angel-4	Jonathan-3
Anthony-1	Jordan-5
Antonio-10	José-4
Austin-5	Joseph-2
Benjamin-3	Joshua-1
Blake-10	Juan-7
Brandon-3	Julian-7
Brayden-8	Justin-5
Brian-8	Kaden-10
Bryan-7	Kevin-4
Caden-10	Kyle-8
Caleb-4	Landon-5
Cameron-6	Liam-10
Carlos-7	Logan-2
Carson-9	Lucas-6
Carter-8	Luis-7
Charles-6	Luke-5
Chase-9	Mason-4
Christian-3	Matthew-1
Christopher-1	Michael-1
Cole-9	Miguel-9
Connor-6	Nathan-5
Daniel-1	Nathaniel-7
David-2	Nicholas-2
Devin-10	Noah-2
Diego-6	Owen-6
Dominic-9	Richard-10
Dylan-3	Robert-5
Elijah-3	Ryan-2
Eric-8	Samuel-3
Ethan-1	Sean-7
Evan-5	Sebastian-8
Gabriel-3	Steven-9
Gavin-4	Thomas-6
Hayden-8	Timothy-10
Henry-10	Tristan-9
Hunter-6	Tyler-2
Ian-9	William-1
Isaac-5	Wyatt-9
Isaiah-4	Xavier-8
Jack-4	Zachary-4

GIRLS' NAMES

Aaliyah-10	Jordan-10
Abigail-1	Julia-4
Addison-3	Kaitlyn-5
Alexa-4	Katelyn-7
Alexandra-4	Katherine-4
Alexis-2	Kayla-3
Allison-5	Kaylee-5
Alyssa-2	Kimberly-6
Amelia-9	Kylie-7
Andrea-6	Lauren-3
Angelina-5	Layla-10
Anna-3	Leah-7
Ariana-8	Lillian-4
Arianna-8	Lily-4
Ashley-2	Mackenzie-6
Aubrey-10	Madeline-8
Audrey-7	Madison-1
Autumn-10	Makayla-5
Ava-1	Maria-5
Avery-6	Mariah-9
Brianna-2	Mary-9
Brooke-5	Maya-6
Brooklyn-7	Megan-6
Caroline-9	Melanie-9
Chloe-2	Mia-2
Claire-9	Michelle-8
Destiny-4	Morgan-4
Elizabeth-2	Natalia-10
Ella-3	Natalie-2
Emily-1	Nevaeh-5
Emma-1	Nicole-8
Evelyn-7	Olivia-1
Faith-7	Paige-8
Gabriella-5	Rachel-5
Gabrielle-7	Rebecca-10
Gianna-10	Riley-6
Grace-2	Samantha-1
Hailey-3	Sara-8
Haley-8	Sarah-2
Hannah-1	Savannah-3
Isabel-9	Sofia-6
Isabella-1	Sophia-1
Isabelle-9	Stephanie-7
Jada-10	Sydney-4
Jasmine-3	Taylor-3
Jayla-10	Trinity-7
Jennifer-6	Valeria-9
Jessica-4	Vanessa-8
Jenna-9	Victoria-3
Jocelyn-8	Zoe-6

Bunco!

All you need for this game is three dice and at least two people to play. First, for each player, draw a score sheet that looks like the one below.

The first player rolls for 1s. Each time that player rolls a 1, he makes a tally mark next to the 1 on his score sheet. The first player rolls until no 1s are rolled, and then passes the dice to the next player. That player rolls for 1s until no 1s are rolled, makes a tally mark for each 1 rolled, and then passes the dice to the next player. The first player to reach 21 tally marks is the winner, and marks a tally mark in the WINS row. The other players put a tally mark in the LOSSES row. Then, you start again, but you roll for 2s.

If you roll three of a kind of any number EXCEPT the number you're trying to roll, it's called a Binco. For example, if you're rolling for 1s and roll three 5s, you get a Binco. A Binco is worth five tally points,

(put them next to the number you're rolling for) and you get to put a tally mark in the Binco row and keep rolling. If you roll three of the number you're trying to roll, you get a Bunco. For example, if you were rolling for 1s and you roll three of them, you say, "Bunco!" That round is over because the player who gets Bunco automatically wins and gets to put a tally mark in the Bunco row and one next to "wins." The other players have to mark losses. After a Bunco, move on to the next number.

When you've rolled for numbers 1 through 6, count up your Wins and see who's the BIG winner. If there's a tie, count your Buncos. The person with the most wins. Still tied? Count Bincos. Still, still tied? Have a roll-off, or call it a tie and start a new game.

Player 1's Name

1
2
3
4
5
6

Wins
Losses
Bincos
Buncos

Welcome to **Cookie Cutter Neighborhood**

Your family is moving to a brand new neighborhood! (Didn't you get the memo?) Unfortunately, all the houses in your 'hood look the same. Draw or color them to make them look a little different so Mom doesn't park in the wrong garage.

What's the name of your neighborhood? Draw a line from one word in the first column, through a word in the second column, to connect to a word in the third column to find your neighborhood's fancy name.

Whispering	River	Downs
Desert	Cliffe	Place
Fern	Field	Park
Autumn	Wynd	Glen
North	Breeze	Cove
Briar	Dale	Towne
Oak	Forest	Landing
Maple	Woods	Farms
Spring	Tree	Gate
Golden	Lake	Chase
Ocean	Creek	Haven
South	Stream	Valley
West	Mountain	Hills
Winter	Hill	Estates
East	Pond	Meadows
Summer	Stone	Acres

No Bones About It

Skeletons hold up all kinds of critters (even people) and give their bodies structure. Fossils are just skeletons that aren't being used anymore. Putting bones together shows what the critter that used them may have looked like. Use the bones on these pages to create your own critters. Make it worthy of an installation in a natural history museum.

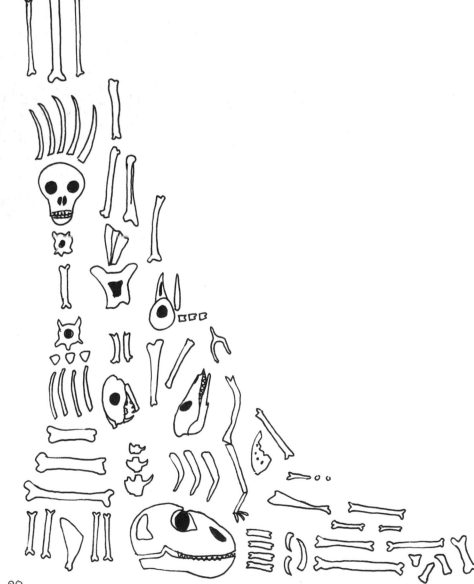

What Are You Selling?

What is each store selling? Fill these windows with the best stuff you've ever seen for sale. Don't forget to add signs and name your stores.

Fact or Fiction?

Have you chewed bubblegum made with spider eggs? Ever seen birds explode? Take this quiz to find out just how good you are at separating fact from fiction. Answers are on page 246.

1. Don't fall asleep with that gum in your mouth! When soft bubblegum was first invented, it contained spider eggs folded into the gum just before it was packaged as a secret ingredient that helped it stay soft. A few chewers woke up with baby spiders—and webs—on their faces.
❏ True   ❏ False

2. A man who got lucky enough to hit the lottery had his luck run out just a couple of hours later when he was hit by a truck.
❏ True   ❏ False

3. Speaking of the lottery, a woman dreamed of a combination of numbers and bought two lottery tickets with that number combo—and won.
❏ True   ❏ False

4. Rice is for the birds—not. Wedding parties are cautioned not to throw rice because if birds ingest the grains, the rice will expand in their stomachs and cause them to die—by exploding.
❏ True   ❏ False

5. The Stanley Cup (the coveted trophy awarded to the winner of the North-American-based National Hockey League) has been left on the side of a road, kicked across an icy canal, stolen twice, and sunk to the bottom of a swimming pool—twice.
❏ True   ❏ False

6. Two children played a funny trick on their parents by having their older sister take them to the grocery store several times to purchase boxes of gelatin for what they said was a school project. The night before a planned party, they poured all of the gelatin into the family swimming pool and turned off the pumps. Guests the next day were surprised when they jumped into the wiggly pool. It took several weeks to repair the pool equipment and get all of the gelatin out of the pool.
❏ True   ❏ False

7. A college student dressed like a football referee (in black and white stripes) tossed out birdseed on a rival college's football field every day for a summer. When the first football game of the fall rolled around and the refs stepped onto the field, it quickly became covered with hungry birds expecting their usual feast, delaying the game for over half an hour.
❏ True   ❏ False

8. Since 1988, a man has been living in an airport in Paris, France.
❒ True   ❒ False

9. After purchasing an old motorcycle, a man did some research on it and realized it had once belonged to rock legend Elvis Presley and was a gift from his wife. He later auctioned it for over a million dollars.
❒ True   ❒ False

10. If you leave a human tooth in a bottle of cola overnight, it will dissolve.
❒ True   ❒ False

11. *Webster's New International Dictionary* mistakenly contained a accidentally made-up, nonexistent word for over five years.
❒ True   ❒ False

12. A 30-foot-high wave of molasses once swept through Boston, Massachusetts, tearing buildings off their foundations and crushing part of a fire department.
❒ True   ❒ False

13. On the spring (vernal) equinox, eggs can be balanced on their ends.
❒ True   ❒ False

14. Some foods and other products that contain red dye are made of ground beetles from South and Central America.
❒ True   ❒ False

15. A cool thing called the Coriolis Effect, which is caused by the rotation of the Earth, means that water runs counterclockwise down drains in the Northern Hemisphere (north of the equator), and clockwise down drains in the Southern Hemisphere.
❒ True   ❒ False

16. Does your kid brother want a cool "tat?" Well, there's now a company that helps parents of babies and small children get tattoos for their tots.
❒ True   ❒ False

17. In Scotland, customers are aiding and abetting a shoplifter who frequently comes into a particular store and steals bags of chips. The customers are paying because the shoplifter can't. It's a seagull.
❒ True   ❒ False

Straight & Curvy

Draw a person or animal using just curvy lines. No straight lines allowed! On the next page, go the straight and narrow by using only straight lines. Which one is more difficult to draw? Which drawing looks more realistic?

Put It in Writing

Some people think that how you write reveals certain things about your personality. Take this handwriting quiz and see what you think. First, write a paragraph on one of the blank pages in the back of the book. It can be about anything, but it needs to be at least 10 lines long, and longer if possible. The more your write the better you'll be able to answer the questions. Next, look at the questions on these two pages and answer them. If you write some letters two different ways, answer the question according to how you think you write the letter most often. Remember that this is just for fun! Don't take the results too seriously. Answers on page 247.

1. How large is your writing? Measure the height of the lowercase letters. Are they:
    a) Smaller than this? _____

    b) Medium (about this height)? _____

    c) Large (about this height or higher)? _____

I LIKE PIE.

2. Look at the sentences you wrote. Do they:

    a) stay straight? _____

    b) run "uphill" a little like this? _____

    c) run "uphill" a lot? _____

    d) run "downhill" a little? _____

    e) run "downhill" a lot? _____

3. Does the writing stay on one line, like this? Or does it move up and down like this?

4. How does your handwriting slant? Does it:
    a) look straight up and down?   b) slant to the right a little?   c) slant to the right a lot?
    d) slant to the left a little?   e) slant to the left a lot?

5. Are your writing lines:
    a) very close together,   or do they   b) have more space   or are they   c) very far
       like this?   between them,   apart,
                                             like this?   like this?

6. Are your letters:
    a) always connected, *like this*?
    b) sometimes connected, *like this*?
    c) always apart, like you're printing, *like this*?

7. Are all of your small letters the same size, **like this**?   Or different sizes, **like this**?

8. Look at your lowercase letter o. Is it:
    a) always closed at the top?   b) always open at the top?

    c) sometimes open?   d) knotted at the top with a loop?

9. Look at how you cross your lowercase letter t. Is the cross:
    a) short?   b) long?   c) high?   d) very high?   e) low?   f) very low?   g) thick?

    h) thin?   i) starting thin and getting thick?   j) starting thick and getting thin?   k) slanting up?

    l) slanting down?

10. Look at your f, g, p, q, and y. Are the loops on the bottom:
    a) very long?   b) very short?   c) very wide?   d) looped in knots?

    e) not looped, but still moving to the right?

11. Look at your uppercase letters B, D, and G. Are they:
    a) wider at the top   or   b) wider at the bottom?

12. Look at all of your uppercase letters. Are they:
    a) like printed letters?   b) like your lowercase letters, except bigger?

    c) Big and rough, with lots of swirls?

13. Look at the dots over your lowercase letter i. Are they:
    a) low?   b) high?   c) to the left?   d) to the right?   e) heavy and dark?   f) light?

    g) shaped like a circle or some other cool shape?   i) missing?

14. Look at your letters with top loops: b, d, f, h, k, l. Are the loops:
    a) low?   b) high?   c) wide?   d) made without loops?   e) made with printed letters?

    f) tied in a knot?

Metamorphosis

Metamorphosis means a total change of physical form.

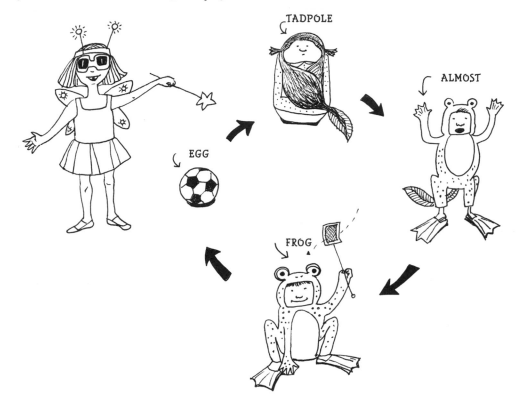

Butterflies, beetles, and frogs do it, now it's your turn. Make up your own creatures, and show how they change from one thing to another.

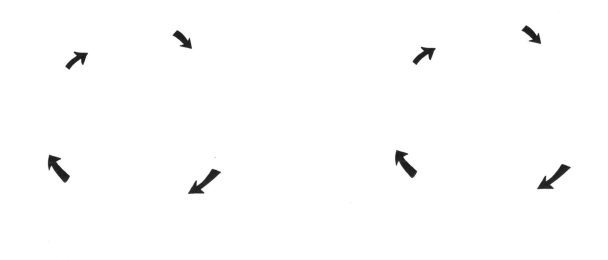

Proverb Completion

The saying you know is "Early to bed, early to rise, makes you healthy, wealthy, and wise." See if you can fill in the blanks to complete these clichéd proverbs. Answers on page 248.

Laughter is the best _____

A bird in the hand _____

Don't count your chickens _____

No news is _____

Don't look a gift horse _____

What goes around _____ .

Every cloud has _____ .

The more things change, _____ .

The early bird catches _____ .

Good fences make _____ .

Measure twice _____ .

When life gives you lemons, _____ .

If at first you don't succeed, _____ .

Actions speak louder than _____ .

If you can't beat 'em, _____ .

You can't judge a book _____ .

Birds of a feather _____ .

Proverb Corruption

Okay, so you did the proverbs correctly (we hope). But instead of "Early to bed, early to rise, makes you healthy, wealthy, and wise," what about "Early to bed, early to rise, until you have enough money to do otherwise!" Finish off these same proverbs to make them funny. And no, they don't have to rhyme.

A bird in the hand _____ .

Don't count your chickens _____ .

No news _____ .

Don't look a gift horse _____ .

What goes around _____ .

Every cloud has _____ .

The more things change _____ .

The early bird _____ .

Good fences make _____ .

Measure twice _____ .

When life gives you lemons, _____ .

If at first you don't succeed, _____ .

Actions speak louder than _____ .

If you can't beat 'em _____ .

You can't judge a book _____ .

Birds of a feather _____ .

Give Ants a Chance

This thing that looks like a maze is really the underground part of an ant colony. Draw the residents. Remember, lots of ants live in a colony, so pack it full!

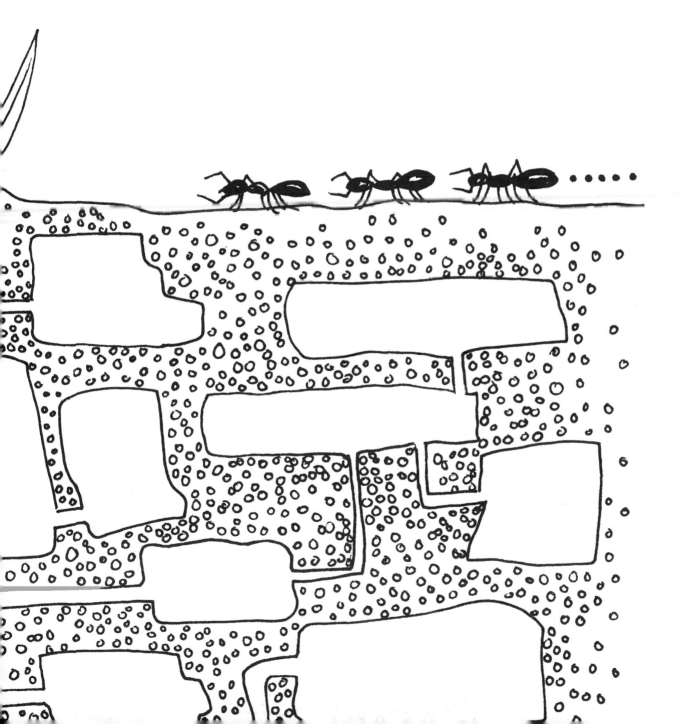

The Next Text Thing

Got a cell phone? If you do, perhaps you're allowed to send text messages to your friends. Since the screen is so small, people have invented a ton of shortcuts for words and phrases so you can type more, faster, and in a smaller space. So, what's your text message IQ? Find out by writing the longer version under each text message abbreviation below. Answers on page 248.

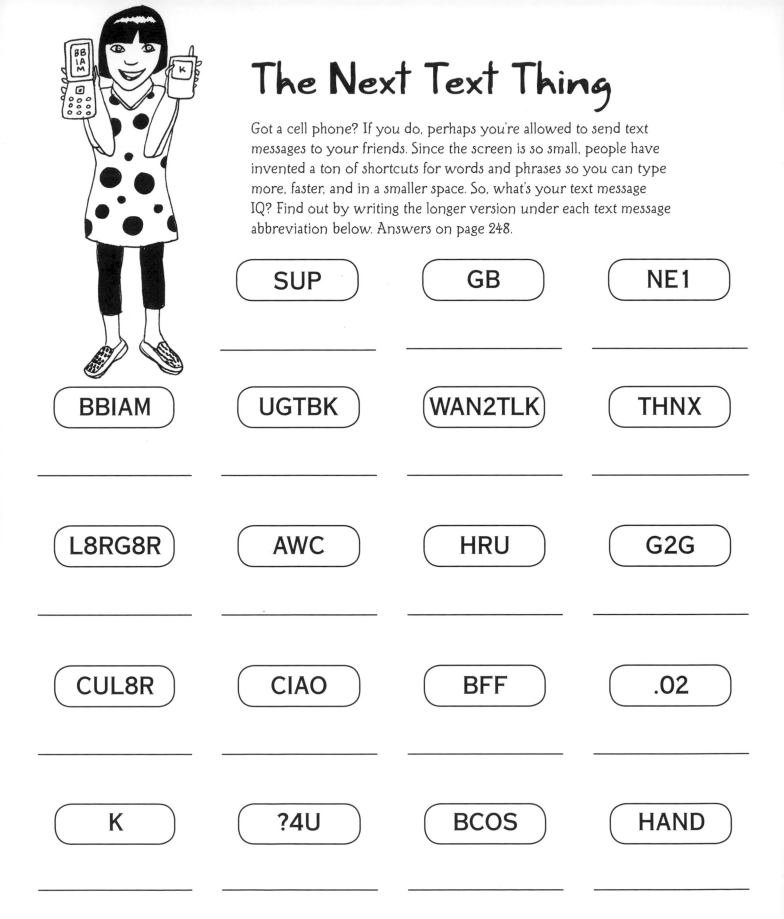

SUP

_____

GB

_____

NE1

_____

BBIAM

_____

UGTBK

_____

WAN2TLK

_____

THNX

_____

L8RG8R

_____

AWC

_____

HRU

_____

G2G

_____

CUL8R

_____

CIAO

_____

BFF

_____

.02

_____

K

_____

?4U

_____

BCOS

_____

HAND

_____

BHL8	EZY	IDK	IMHO
_____	_____	_____	_____

JK	IG2R	KEYA	PU
_____	_____	_____	_____

ROFL	GR8	IC	BIBI
_____	_____	_____	_____

Don't stop with these. Make up some of your own!

Haunted House

Oh no! You have been hired to design a new ride at an amusement park. It's going to be a fabulous haunted house. First, pick the name from the list of words below.

Dusty
Grungy
Pit
Dreary
Rusty
Smelly
Nightmare

Oozing
Harsh
Crusty
Slimy
Grimy
Scary
Cavern

Cold
Creepy
Junky
Ditch
Gully
Slippery
Haunted

Valley
Hole
Moaning
Drain
Dark
Mud
Cave

Crevice
Mine
Gutter
Stinky
Grave
Marsh
Swamp

After you pick your name, think about what your haunted house should look like. What kinds of monsters belong in it? Make a list of what you want to see in your haunted house:

_____

Now draw your haunted house. Make it as creepy as possible.

Inspiration Caption

We write 'em, you draw 'em funny! Draw some cartoons to go with these captions.

My parents think they know what "cool" looks like.

Ready or not, here I come!

Is this what they mean by,
"Be on your best behavior?"

Now, that's what I call a super power!

That is SO last year.

"Must . . . reach . . . utility . . . belt!"

Is it raining down there yet?

Swamp

Rats

Try to round up the rats before the gators get you. Find a friend to play this game with you. Each of you needs a pencil and a game board (rip a page of grids out for your friend). Here's how you play:

1. First, both players should draw five of the gator symbols on your grid (see the gator below). On the sample below, the gators are at A4 , B7, B9, D10, and F1. Make sure your opponent can't see your swamp!

2. Next, draw 10 swamp rats (see symbol below). Make a note of where those are, too. The ones on the sample board below are at A6, C2, C8, D3, D5, E1, E7, E9, F3, and F10.

3. The object of the game is to guess where your opponent's swamp rats are before getting chomped by the gators. Choose one player to go first. That person guesses a space on the opponent's grid. If the space holds a swamp rat, the opponent says, "Swamp Rat!" If the space holds a gator, he says, "Gator!" If there's nothing on the space, he says, "Nothing."

4. The player who's guessing should draw an X over the spaces he guesses. After one guess, it's the other player's turn. The player who finds 10 swamp rats (without finding all five gators) first, wins. Each player should keep track of where he has guessed and of how many gators and rats he's found.

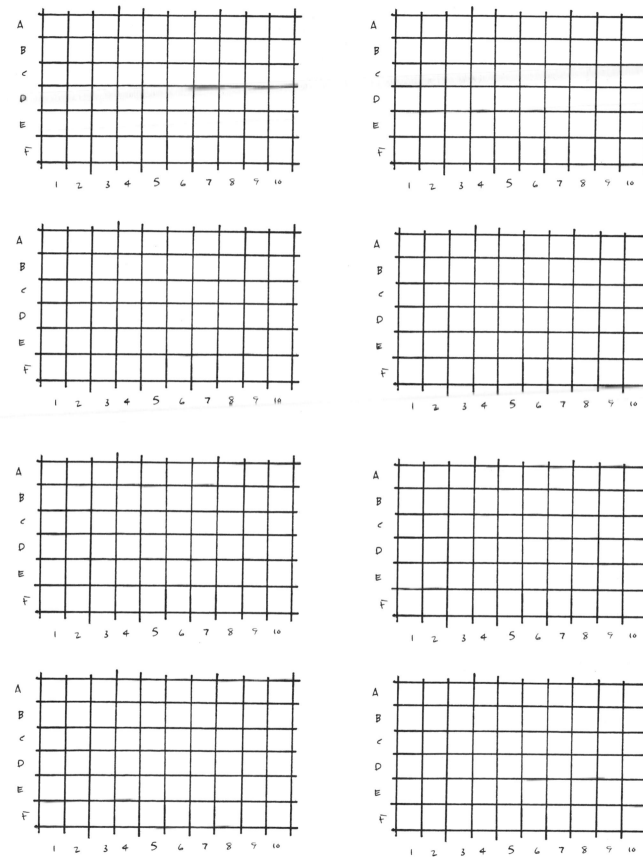

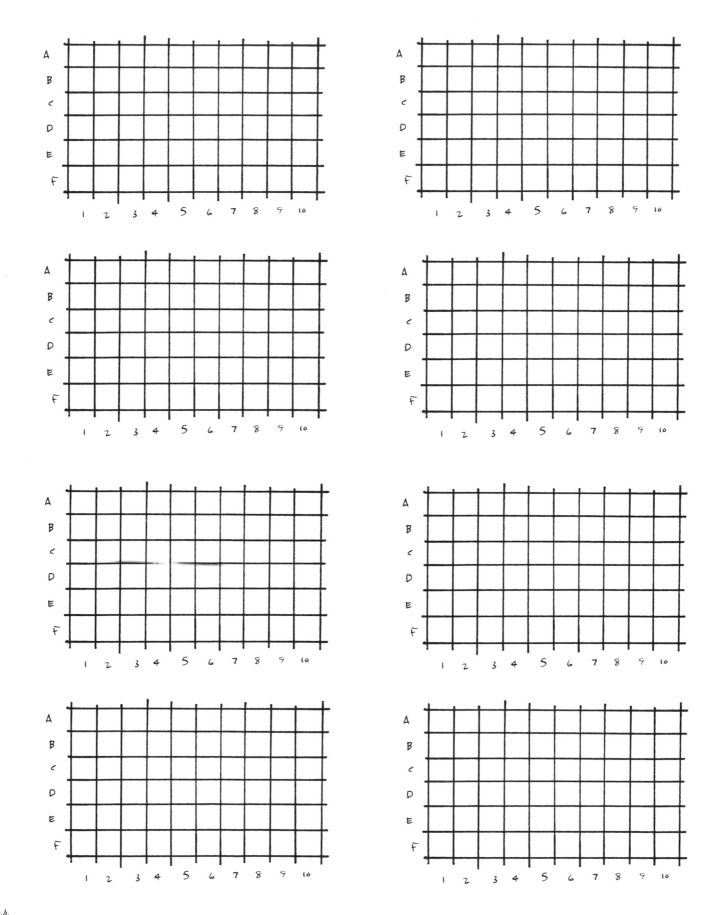

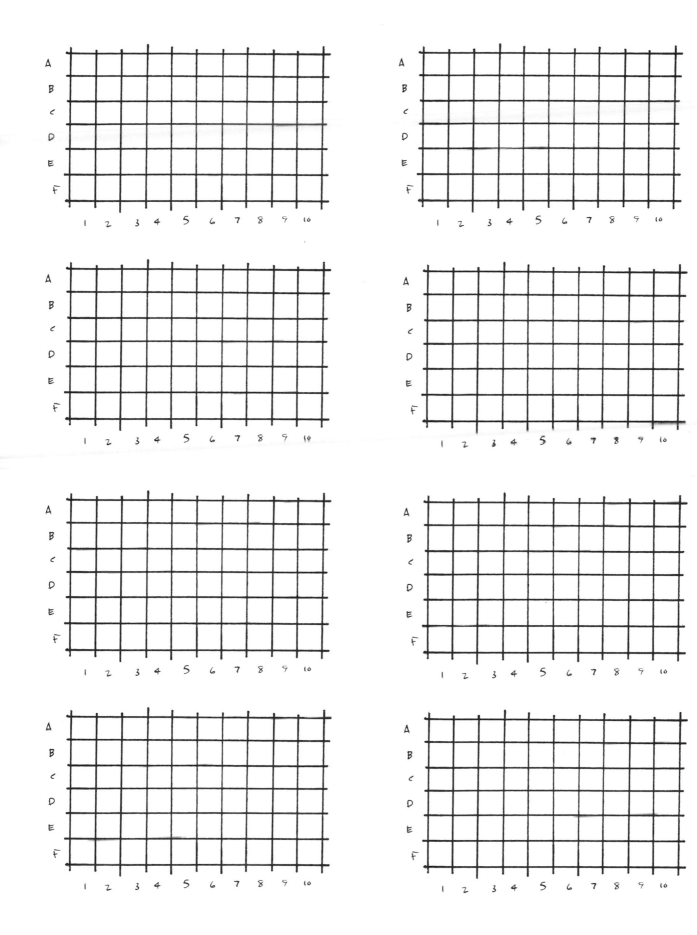

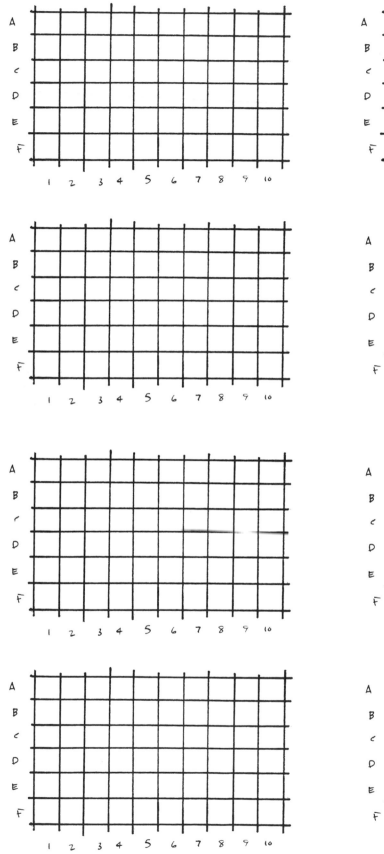
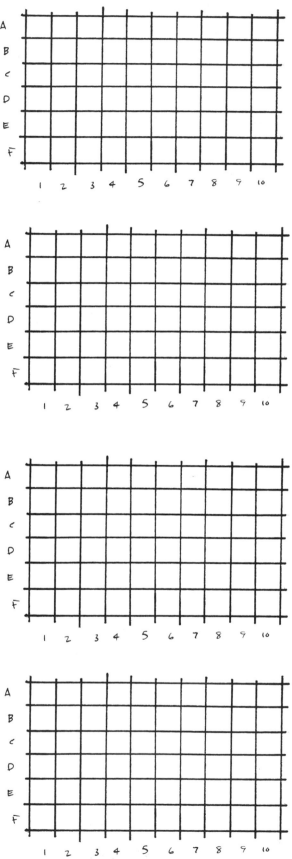

46

Hands-On

Here are some weird things to do with your hands.

Nondominant Writing

Most people are either right- or left-handed. Although some people can use either hand for things like throwing, you probably write with only one hand. Try writing with your nondominant hand and see how your handwriting looks. Pretty sloppy, right? Practice for a week and compare. Is your handwriting getting any neater? Next, try drawing any of the illustrations on this page with your nondominant hand. By the way, this isn't just silly fun. Nondominant writing is considered a good way to exercise your brain.

Dead Fingers

Get one of your friends to put her hand against yours, palm-to-palm, with your fingers spread out. Then, rub both of your index fingers using the index finger and thumb of your other hand. The fingers will feel "dead" because you expect to be able to feel the rubbing on the other side of your hand. Ew!

Shaking Hands

When you meet someone, shaking hands is a part of the impression you make on them. To do a regular handshake, firmly (but not painfully) grasp the right hand of someone in front of you, palm-to-palm, and move your hand up and down once. There are other, more casual handshakes: fist bumping (making a fist and gently tapping your knuckles against your friend's), high- or low-fiving/slapping hands, or rotating your hand, locking thumbs, and then pulling your hands apart, fingers last. Make up some secret handshakes and do them with your friends.

Turn Art on Its Head

Think you can't draw? Think again. If you want to draw what you *see*, sometimes it's easier if you look at each line, not at the whole picture. The picture below is upside down, obviously. Draw the picture you see on the facing page. Instead of looking at the whole picture as you draw, try to just look at each line as you draw it. (That should be easier since the drawing is upside down and it's harder to look at the whole picture.) When you're finished, just turn this book upside down and see how you did. You might surprise yourself!

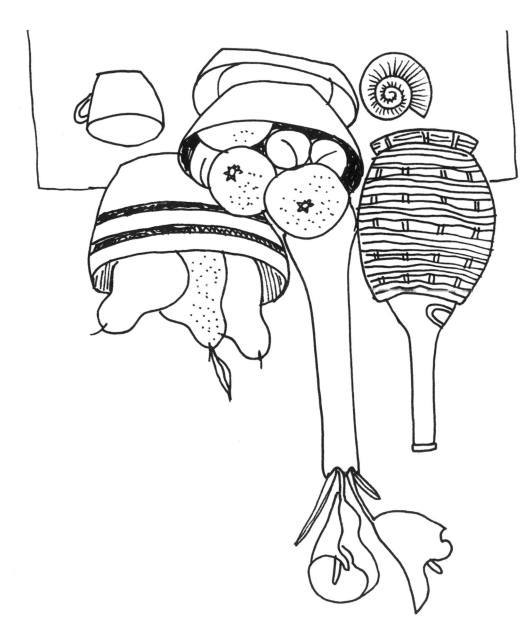

What's Not to Like?

So, your friends and your parents probably like lots of things about you. If your friends didn't, they wouldn't be your friends. And your parents have to like you, right? But what is there to like about you? Answer these questions and add up the points to find out! See your results on page 249.

1. Which one of these pets would you most like to have?
   - a. puppy (1)
   - b. cockatoo (4)
   - c. chimpanzee (3)
   - d. pony (5)
   - e. jaguar (6)
   - f. snake (2)

2. If you're trying to listen in class and your friends are making too much noise for you to hear the teacher, what do you do?
   - a. nothing (1)
   - b. move closer to the front of the room (2)
   - c. throw balled-up pieces of paper at them (3)
   - d. ask them to be quiet (4)
   - e. raise your hand and ask a question—loudly (6)
   - f. get mad and pout (5)

3. At recess, one of your friends gets in a fight with someone else. What do you do?
   - a. help your friend out in the fight (5)
   - b. cry (1)
   - c. try to talk them out of fighting (4)
   - d. ask, "Who do you think will win?" (6)
   - e. throw water on them (3)
   - f. leave before you get hurt (2)

4. Which kind of television show would you most like to be on?
   - a. a public television show (2)
   - b. a talk show (5)
   - c. a show about your pet (1)
   - d. a cartoon (3)
   - e. a game show (6)
   - f. a talent contest (4)

5. What do you want to be when you grow up?
   - a. nurse (1)
   - b. president of a big company (6)
   - c. guide at a museum (2)
   - d. teacher (4)
   - e. singer (5)
   - f. comedian (3)

6. You didn't turn in a science fair project. What is most likely to be the reason?
   - a. your sister had to go to the hospital and you wanted to go with her (1)
   - b. the truth—whatever that is (4)
   - c. your experiment yielded some very unexpected results and you wanted to do another trial to see if you could dupliucate them (2)
   - d. you were so worried about what your teacher would think that you were afraid to turn it in (6)
   - e. your dog ate it (3)
   - f. you don't like science, so you didn't do it (5)

7. Which of these is most important to you?
- a. getting a summer job or an allowance (6)
- b. school (2)
- c. family (1)
- d. sleep (3)
- e. friends (5)
- f. music or another hobby (4)

8. Someone you know falls in the hallway. What do you do?
- a. offer a hand to pull her up (5)
- b. ask, "Are you okay?" (4)
- c. help gather her things and walk her to the office so you can tell the principal who tripped her (6)
- d. get a bandage for her skinned knee (1)
- e. laugh with her (3)
- f. get a teacher to help her (2)

9. What's your favorite kind of book?
- a. history (2)
- b. funny novel with a happy ending (1)
- c. puzzles and games (4)
- d. nonfiction (6)
- e. scary (5)
- f. comic book (3)

10. Where is your favorite place to eat?
- a. pizza place with singing waiters (3)
- b. game room and snack bar (5)
- c. a grown-up restaurant—you like gourmet food (6)
- d. a place that serves healthy food (4)
- e. your house, because your mom is a great cook (1)
- f. unusual ethnic food, such as Thai or Moroccan (2)

Clown Car

Question: How many clowns will fit in this car?
Answer: That's totally up to you—draw them in!

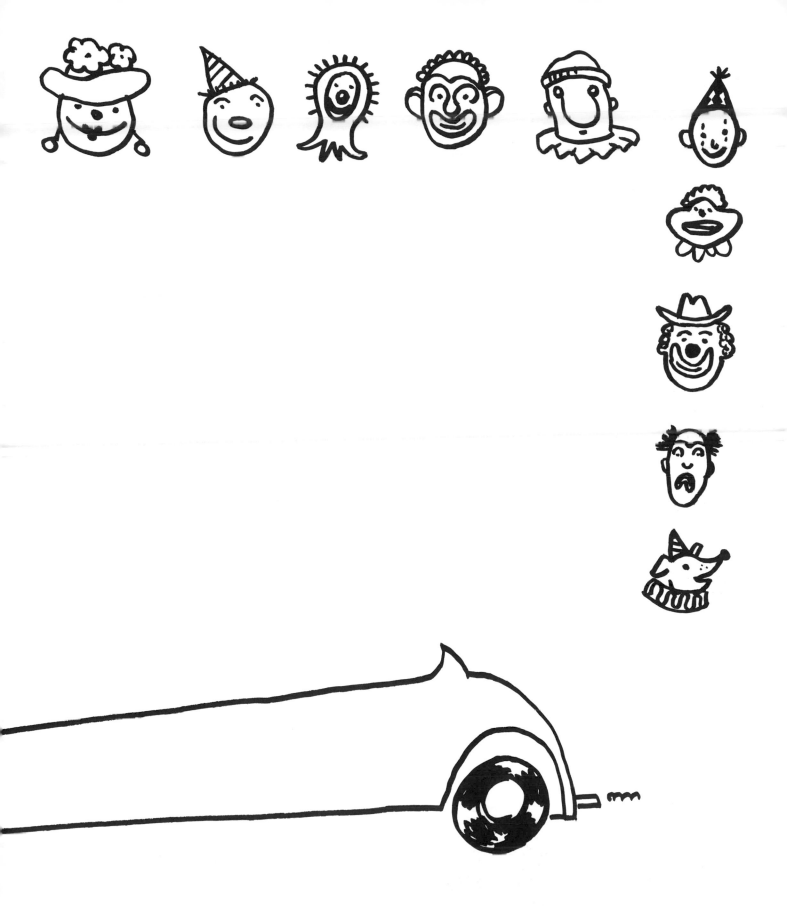

Foot-ology

Headache? Stuffy nose? Try rubbing, uh, your feet. People who believe in reflexology claim that there are certain places on your feet that correspond to different organs and other body parts. By rubbing these places on your feet, reflexologists think that you can relieve pain or at least reduce stress in the corresponding part of your body.

You can do a little experiment to see whether or not you respond to reflexology. On the following page is a "map" of your feet. The next time you have a minor ache or pain, figure out where it hurts and then look up the matching area on the bottoms of your feet. Rub that place for a while (at least 15 minutes) and then see if your ache or pain goes away. If you feel better, great! If not, well, at least you gave yourself a nice foot rub.

Triangle Touchdown

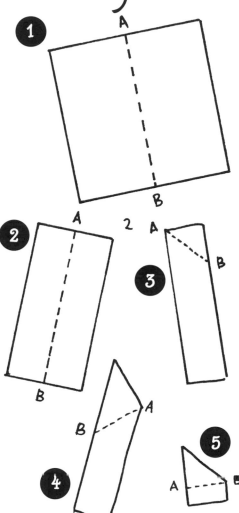

You can play football without a pigskin, shoulder pads, or a field. Play it with a sheet of paper and a table with straight edges, instead. First, get a piece of printer paper. Fold it in half longways (1), and then cut or tear it down the fold. Take one of the pieces and repeat (2). Hold one of the four pieces you now have vertically and fold a top corner down (3) to meet the side, to make a triangle (4). Keep folding it, making triangles, until you reach the bottom. Tuck the extra paper at the bottom into the pocket that was formed by all of the folding (5). This is your football.

Now, grab a friend and sit on opposite sides of the table. Start by kicking off. Put the football flat on the table near your edge. Flick the triangle football toward the other side of the table. You have a total of four chances to flick the football so it's hanging off your opponent's edge of the table without it falling off. If the football doesn't reach the other side of the table, your friend gets to try to flick it back toward your table edge. If at any time, the football falls off the table, the other "team" kicks off. Each touchdown worth six points. (You can test this by running your finger along the edge of the table to see if the football moves.)

If you get a touchdown, you then get to kick a field goal. Get your friend to hold her fingers like the kid below. Hold the football between your finger and thumb, on your edge of the table (or up in the air), and flick it with your other index finger. If it sails through the goalposts, you get an extra point, and it's the other players turn to kickoff. Decide on a score to play to, and have fun.

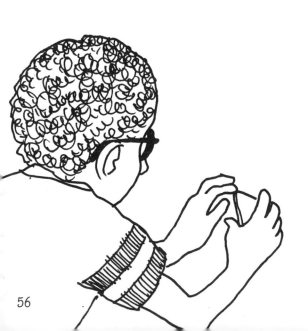

drowssorC elzzuP

You've done plenty of crosswords. Well, here's your chance to do one backwards. Well, sort of. We have given you the answers, you have to come up with the clues. After you write your clues on the next page, let your friend use them to try to fill in the blank crossword grid.

Hints for making good crossword clues:
· Don't make them too obvious. For example, if the answer is Dalmatian, instead of using "spotted dog" as the clue, you might use, "Firefighter's best friend," since Dalmatians used to live at firehouses.
· Try asking questions with your clues. For Dalmatian, you could say, "Dog easily spotted?" That makes the friend who's filling out the clues wonder if you mean spotted, or easily seen. Clever, huh?

Crossword Clues

Write your clues here.

ACROSS

2. _____

5. _____

7. _____

8. _____

9. _____

11. _____

12. _____

DOWN

1. _____

2. _____

3. _____

4. _____

6. _____

10. _____

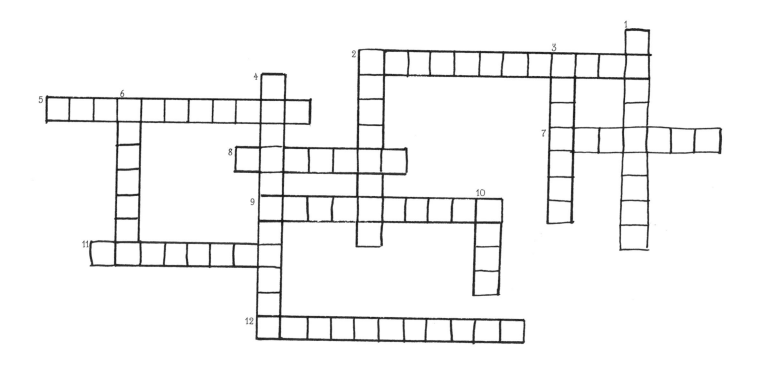

BEghILOSZ

Beghilosz is a name used for spelling words on a calculator. Grab a calculator and type the numbers 250714938. Turn the calculator upside down and you've spelled:

B	E	g	h	I	L	O	S	Z
8	3	9	4	1	7	0	5	2

You can see that each letter is really a number: 2507146938. The tricky part is that you have to turn the calculator upside down to see the words.

Here's a story for you to figure out. Grab a calculator and do a little math. Then write the word in the blank. Answers on page 249.

Today was going to be a (54 x 17)_____ day. I was in a hurry to go to a carnival after school but had a map test to study for first. I had left my social studies book at home. So I got my (20111 + 17968) _____ out of my closet, and looked up the places I needed to know for my map test, like (0.140)_____. Then, my phone rang. It was my friend (28867 x 11)_____. She was finished with homework and wanted to go to the carnival and (7272 ÷ 9)_____ for apples, for some reason. I said sure and met her outside. We ran into our friend (8156 + 225 - 663)_____ and all went together. First, we went to the (3 x 221)_____ toss. I shattered both of my (461 x 13)_____ but my friends did pretty well. We stopped by the petting zoo where they had some (4417 x 2 x 2 x 2)_____ some (977 + 678 + 445 + 998 - 885 + 2811 + 314)_____, some (637 x 9)_____, and some (3 x 467 x 4)_____. We went on some crazy rides. On a roller coaster called the Crazy (457589.09 + 3785.91)_____, I got so dizzy all I could do was (37501596 ÷ 99_____ away and try not to (167 x 21)_____ my lunch. I was afraid my brain would (25600 ÷

8)_____ out of my ears. We were hungry and could hear the (300,000 + 70,000 + 2,000 + 200 + 10 + 5)_____ of fries, but my friends wanted (1772569 x 3)_____. Finally, we found the place where (28867 x 11)_____ could (202 + 202 + 202 + 202)_____ for apples and win a prize. She put on a (204.5 x 4)_____ and some (1,017,489 + 86,753 + 3,236,701 + 77,186 + 58,833 + 672,801 + 199,301 + 27,542)_____ and watched as they used a (584 x 6)_____ to refill the barrel. Then she stuck her head under water, opened her mouth, and tried to (4166866 ÷ 11) _____ an apple. Soon, she lifted her head and shouted with (844 x 4)_____. She got an apple! She went to get her prize. The man running the game said, "You are not (1400599 x 3 x 3 x 3)_____ to win because you have to be under age 5, but we'll make an exception. You have your choice of a blow-up (0.0791)_____ or a set of doll (10609 x 5) _____. (28867 x 11)_____ laughed and took the (0.0791)_____ for her little brother. We left to look for some food to fill our (5999913 − 682175)_____.

Frame-Up

Say you own an art gallery and it's your job to decide how to display the art. One thing you may have to decide is how to frame the artwork. Think about art you have seen, and draw frames around these pictures.

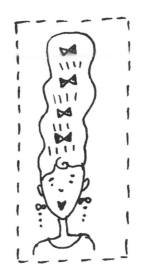

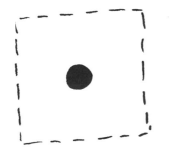

Random Stuff about You

Answer the questions below. Then, ask a friend the same questions. Why? Well, you might find out something cool you didn't know before. Or something completely useless.

1. Were you named after anyone?

   _____

2. When was the last time you really cried?

   _____

3. Do you like your handwriting? Why or why not?

   _____

4. How's your relationship between you and your siblings?

   _____

5. If you were another person, would you be friends with you?

   _____

6. Do you use sarcasm a lot?

   _____

7. Do you still have any baby teeth?

   _____

8. Would you bungee jump? Sky dive? Ride a motorcycle?

   _____

9. Favorite lunch meat?

   _____

10. Favorite cereal? Why?

   _____

11. Do you untie your shoes when you take them off?

_____

12. Do you think you're strong? Smart? Funny?

_____

13. Favorite ice cream? Why?

_____ mint chocolate-chip _____

14. What is the first thing you notice about people?

_____

15. Would you rather walk, ride a bike, or drive in a car?

_____

16. What is your least favorite thing about yourself?

_____

17. Whom do you miss the most?

_____

18. What's your favorite color in clothes?

_____

19. What was the last thing that you ate?

_____

20. What music are you listening to these days?

_____

21. If you were a crayon, what color would you be?

_____

22. Favorite smells?

_____

23. Who is your favorite person to talk to on the phone?

_____

24. Favorite sports to play?

Soccer
_____

25. Scary movies or happy endings?

Scary movies
_____

26. What was the last movie you watched?

_____

27. Summer or winter?

Summer
_____

28. Favorite dessert?

ice cream
_____

29. What book are you reading now?

_____

30. What's your screen saver?

_____

31. What was the last thing you watched on TV?

_____

32. Favorite sound?

_____

33. Cartoons or reality TV?

Cartoons
_____

34. What is the farthest you have ever been from home?

_____

35. Do you have a special talent?

_____

36. Where were you born? _Sumy, Ukraine_

_____

37. Do you consider yourself a good student?

_____

38. When you wear a backpack do you put it over both shoulders or only one?

_____

39. What's your favorite game to play? _manhunt_

_____

40. What's your favorite joke?

_____

41. What musical instrument do you wish you could play? _gitar_

_____

42. Favorite sports to watch?

_____

43. Early riser or night owl? _early riser_

_____

44. Lucky number? _3_

_____

45. Which one of your friends' answers do you think will be most like yours?

_____

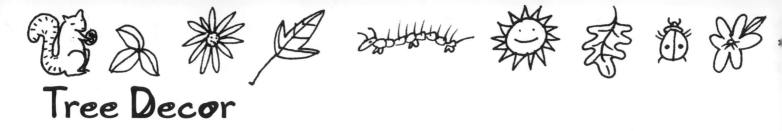

Tree Decor

Add leaves, fruits, nuts, kids, cats, swings, even your Granny, if you wish.

Kitchen Impossible

You may be a great cook, or you may not even know how to open a can of beans, but either way, we bet you won't be able to find all of these gadgets in your cabinets. Give yourself five point if you know what it is, and five additional points if you can find one in your kitchen. Answers are on page 249.

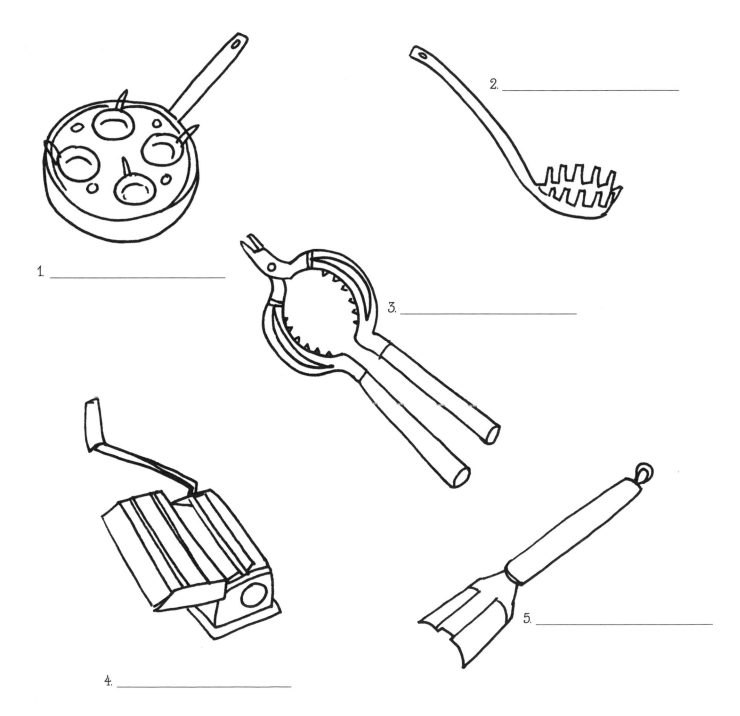

1. _____

2. _____

3. _____

4. _____

5. _____

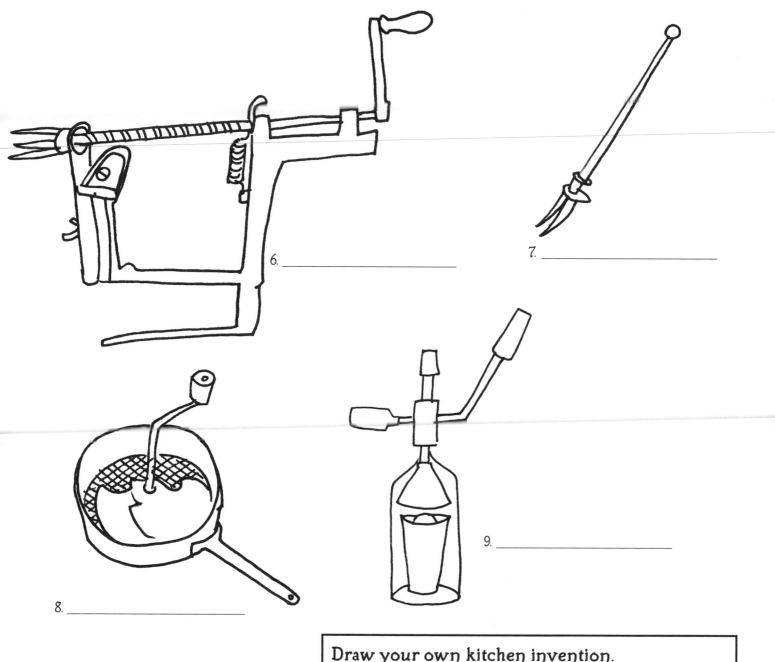

6. _____

7. _____

8. _____

9. _____

Draw your own kitchen invention.

Senri-me, Senryu

You have probably heard of haiku, the Japanese form of poetry that's often written about nature, that doesn't rhyme, and that has a 5-7-5 pattern (5 syllables in the first line, 7 in the second, and 5 in the third), although any short-long-short pattern will work. But have you heard of senryu? It has the same short-long-short pattern as a haiku, but a senryu is usually about human nature and is often funny in a dark or sarcastic way.

See how witty you are by matching the missing final lines to their Senryu poems. See answers on page 249.

Here is an example.

Tomorrow's Thanksgiving.
I love to eat until I'm stuffed.
Oh wait, I'm the turkey.

My mom has three kids.
I am the smartest one of all.

Favorite cereal.
Sugar-frosted sweetie blobs.

I love ice cream cones.
Oops, I dropped it on the ground.

On the crowded bus,
I get to sit near a cute girl

Martians don't exist.
There are no little green men.

I love driving.
I look cool behind the wheel

Who has the stomach flu.

Oh wait, she just has two.

Of Mom's old minivan.

Five-second rule. Yum.

They're fortified with iron.

Except for leprechauns.

Now, try your hand at completing some of your own. We started them, you finish them.

Fuzzy and hairy.
Brush, comb, bathe, dry, clip, trim, shave, sweep.
_____

My brand new cell phone.
Here is my first text message.
"_____"

I like eating pizza.
But not with _____
_____

Creepy animals.
_____

Sleep next to my bed.

I love outer space.
_____

I feel at home there.

Now, write your own.

_____

_____

_____

_____

_____

_____

_____

Alter Egos

Draw your alter ego, your avatar, the REAL you.

Monster Tic Tac Toe

Forget about getting three in a row. The rules are pretty much the same but the boards are huge, and you need five in a row (across, down, or diagonally) to win. Here's a hint—don't let your opponent get more than three in a row! Here is a finished game sample for you.

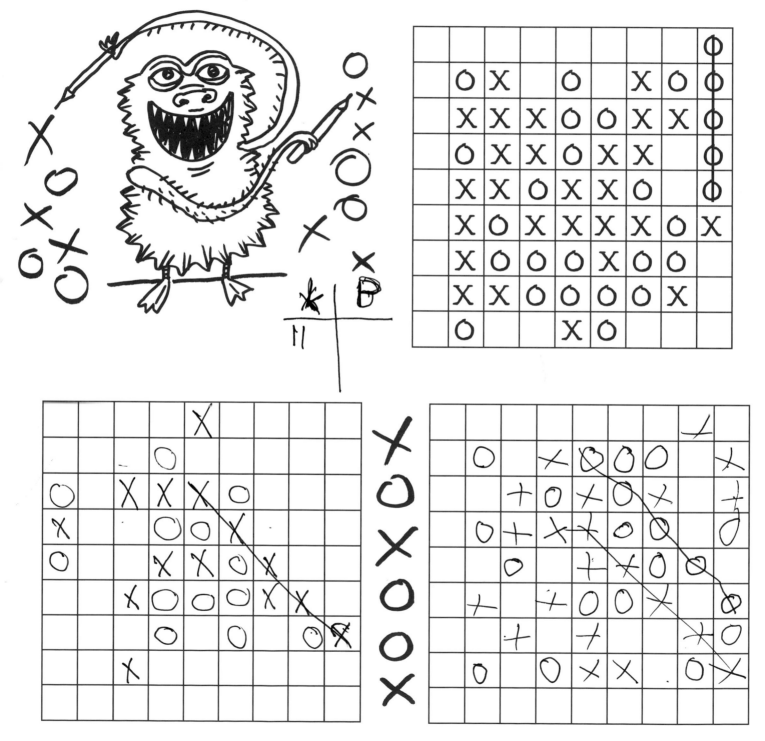

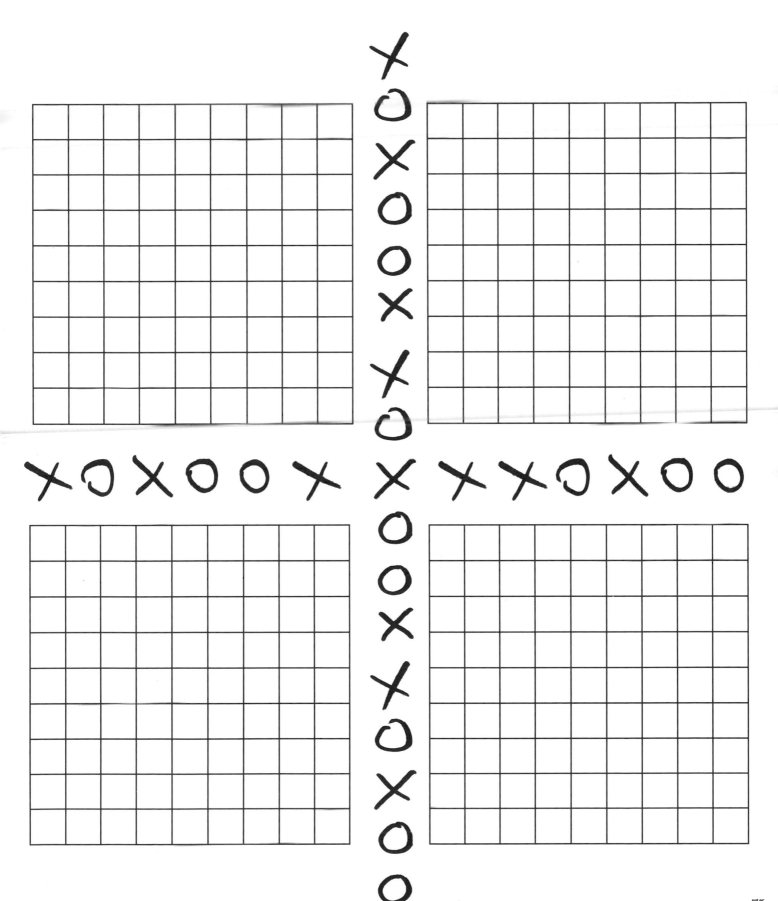

75

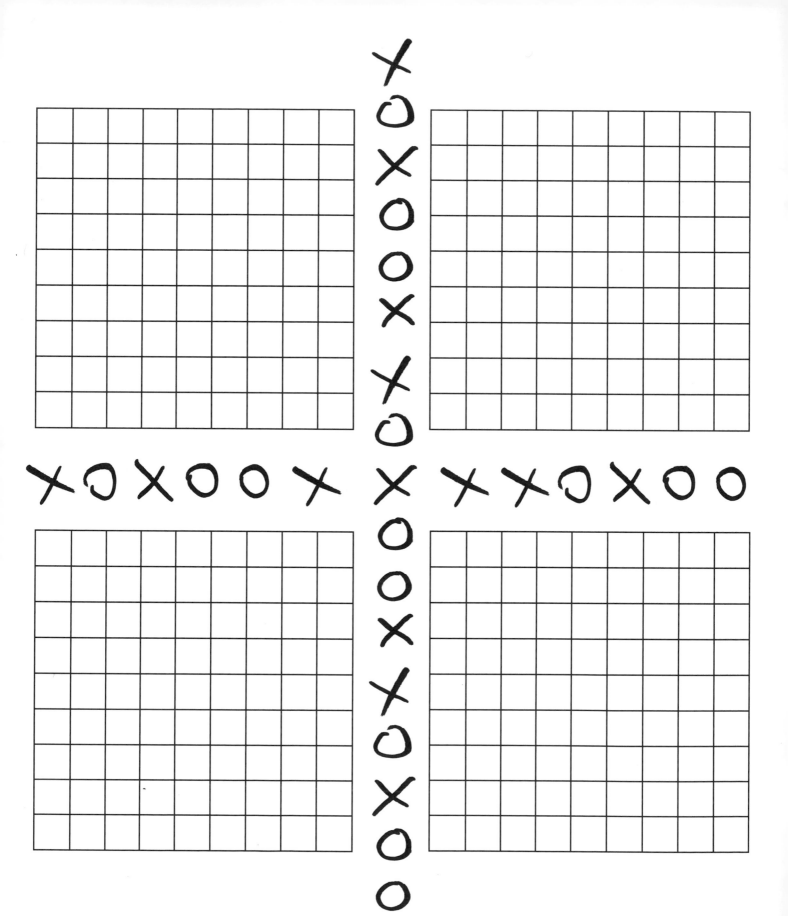

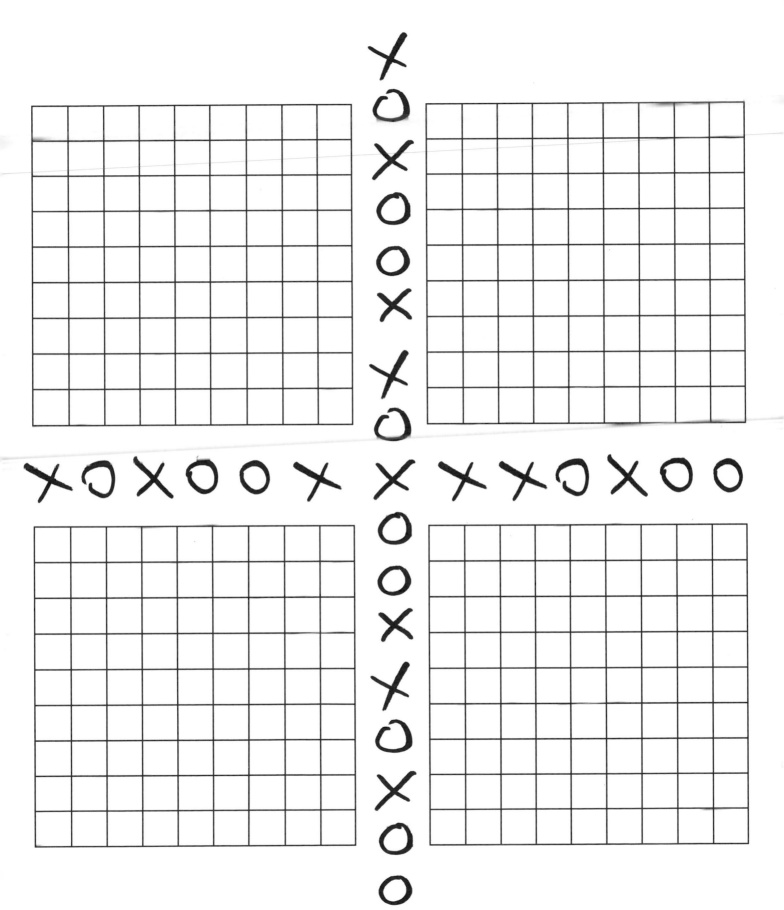

77

All for One (Meaning)

The words in each row all mean the same thing. Some are archaic (not used anymore), some are slang, and others are from different cultures or are in different languages. Can you figure out their meanings? See page 250 for answers. We did the first one for you.

1. pantaloons, dungarees, denims = pants

2. cleric, vicar, mullah _____

3. trainers, sneakers, kicks _____

4. grub, chow, nosh _____

5. folding, readies, green _____

6. gobsmacked, agog, thunderstruck _____

7. jubilent, giddy, pumped _____

8. poppet, shaver, nipper _____

9. crony, cobber, amigo _____

10. beanfeast, fiesta, shindig _____

11. row, donnybrook, scrap _____

12. flummoxed, addled, discombobulated _____

13. piqued, nowty, cheesed _____

14. bugaboo, hitch, scrape _____

15. clam diggers, jodhpurs, kecks _____

Making a Game Plan

On the next two pages, we have provided a great pattern to make your own board game. You've got a start and a finish, and now it's up to you to come up with the theme and the rules. Here are some tips to help you plan your game.

1. You need some different colored pieces so that players can tell themselves apart on the board. You can use different colored stones, coins, or even borrow game pieces from other games.

2. You need either a die or a spinner. You can make a die by drawing dots or writing numbers on a square block.

3. Think of a theme so you can decorate your board. The theme will decide what the board looks like, the name of the game, and maybe some other things. But wait, don't decorate it yet! You need to make a few more decisions.

4. Now, think what's going to be fun about your game. Are you going to answer trivia questions? Sing songs? Do silly things? Spell words? Work math problems? Decode text messages? All of these? Once you decide what will be fun about your game, get some index cards or notes from a note pad. You want at least 50 cards for your games, so pass out a few cards to a few different people, give them directions for what you want them to write (the "fun things" you picked), and tell them to write some cards. They should write the answers upside down on the cards.

5. After you have your cards and your die or spinner and your theme, you can decorate your board. Draw pictures related to the theme. Also, mark some spaces with special directions, like, "Move ahead two spaces," or "Lose a turn."

6. The last thing you need to do is to make some rules. Think about how many people can play, and how you decide who goes first. Since you will be using cards, you need to make a rule about how you move with the cards. The easiest thing to do is to read the card and if you get the answer right, you can roll the die or spin the spinner. You also want to explain how the game is won. Write all of your rules on a sheet of paper. You may have to make some changes as you play, so write the rules in pencil.

7. You may want to cut out the game board pages and laminate them, or tape them to a sheet of cardboard so that the board is less flimsy.

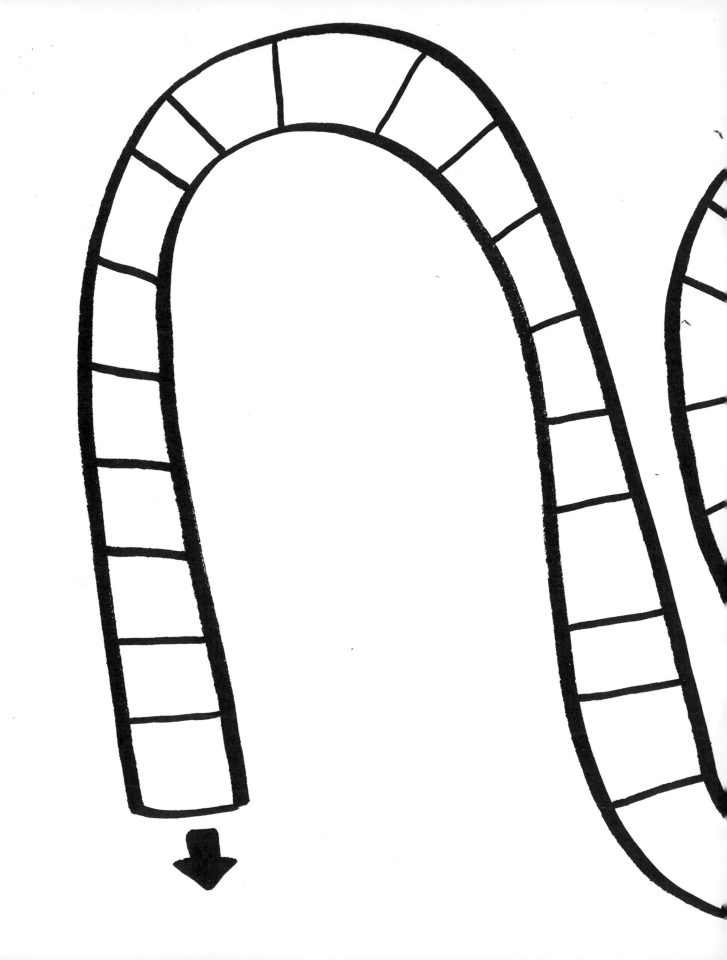

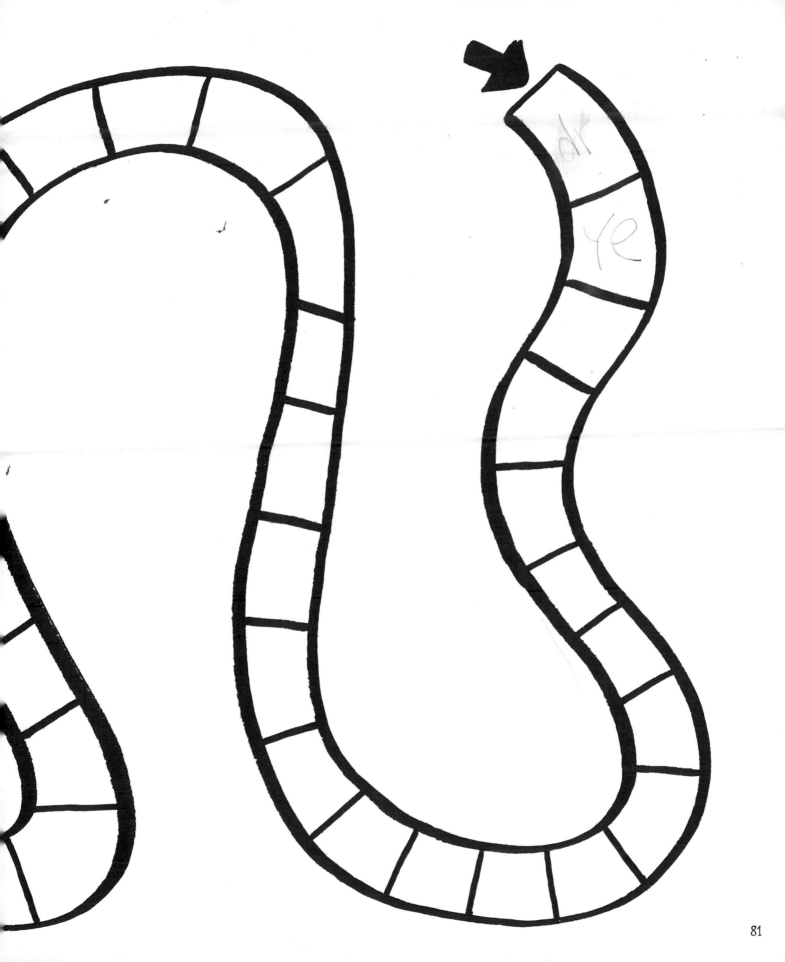

81

Brainbenders

Can you place the numbers 0–10 in the circles so that every three numbers in a straight line add up to 15?

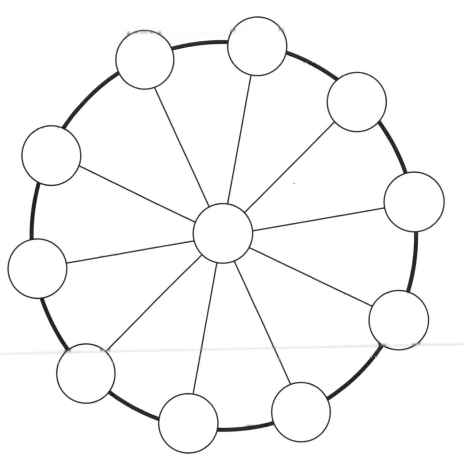

Can you put your pencil on the paper and draw six straight lines that connect all of the dots, without lifting your pencil?

Give up? Turn to page 250.

Eyewitness

Would you make a good eyewitness for an accident, or even a crime scene? You can train your eyes to see more details and your mind to remember them. Start by looking at this picture for five minutes. Then, cover this page and see how many of the questions on the next page you can answer. (No peeking!) Answers on page 250.

Eyewitness Questions

1. How many children are in the line holding hands?
2. Who's wearing sunglasses?
3. What kind of road sign can you see on the pole?
4. A woman is carrying a notebook. What sign is on the notebook cover?
5. What kind of animal is the teacher walking on a leash?
6. What is the mannequin wearing?
7. How many bicycles are in the picture?
8. What are the three people on the bench doing?
9. Which one of these things is NOT in the picture?
   a) trash can b) mailbox c) fire hydrant
10. How many children are in the picture?
11. How many cars are in the picture?
12. Is anyone holding a cup?
13. Describe one item in the trash.
14. How many people are in the picture?
15. Describe the clothing of at least two people.

Draw Your Own Eyewitness

Draw your own detailed picture here and come up with questions for your friends to answer.

Think Big

What's the biggest thing you've ever seen, touched, grew, achieved, or participated in? Draw a picture of this event. Write a caption while you're at it. Big things are worth remembering.

Channel Challenge

OK, so one of the great things about an activity book is that it gets you away from the TV. But hey, the next time you do watch TV, see what you can check off from this list in half an hour. It's a TV scavenger hunt! You can play with a friend if both of you watch different TVs.

____ Someone singing with a microphone.
____ Extra point: Sing the first verse of the song.

____ A commercial for a car.
____ Extra point: What was one feature of the car? _____

____ A dog.
____ Extra point: What kind of dog is it? _____

____ A channel with a ticker across the bottom.

____ A phone number.
____ Extra point: What were the last four digits of the number? _____

____ A game show.
____ Extra point: Are they are giving away a trip? If so, where?_____

____ A commercial for something with A LOT of sugar in it.
____ Extra point: Is it a food you could eat for breakfast?_____

____ An animal you could never have as a pet.
____ Extra point: What kind of animal is it?_____

____ A sport or a game on TV.
____ Extra point: What's the score?_____

____ A weather forecast.
____ Extra point: What kind of weather will you have tomorrow?_____

____ A TV on the TV.
____ Extra point: If the TV on the TV is on, what show is on it?_____

____ A cartoon.
____ Extra point: What is the name of the main cartoon character(s)?_____

____ A rainy or stormy scene.
____ Extra point: If you see lightning or snow, give yourself an extra point.

____ A program with someone speaking another language.
____ Extra point: What language is it? _____

____ An old movie in black & white.
____ Extra point: Has anyone in your family ever seen the movie? (Grandparents count!)

____ Three different people in hats.
____ Extra point: Find three different hats, like a baseball cap, a top hat, and a beret. _____

____ A wild animal in its natural habitat.
____ Extra point: What kind of animal is it? _____

____ A commercial for a toy.
____ Extra point: Give yourself an extra point if you already have that toy.

____ Someone talking into a microphone.
____ Extra point: Give yourself an extra point if the person is interviewing someone.

____ A channel that is all fuzzy—your TV doesn't show it, for some reason.

____ A channel that tells you what is on all the other channels.

____ A car race.
____ Extra point: What's the number of the car in first place? _____

____ People having a conversation in a car.
____ Extra point: Give yourself an extra point if they are in a car chase.

____ Someone brushing her teeth.
____ Extra point: What's the name of the toothpaste? _____

____ Someone making food.
____ Extra point: What is he making? _____
____ Give yourself another point if it's dessert.

____ A channel logo (usually found in one corner of the screen).

____ A news program.

____ A movie about dinosaurs.

List-en Up!

Love to make lists? Then make some!

Write a grocery list of what YOU would buy if you were the main grocery shopper in your house.

1. _____
2. _____
3. _____
4. _____
5. _____
6. _____
7. _____
8. _____
9. _____
10. _____

List your 10 biggest fears.

1. _____
2. _____
3. _____
4. _____
5. _____
6. _____
7. _____
8. _____
9. _____
10. _____

Write a list of 10 names you would like to name your next pet.

1. _____
2. _____
3. _____
4. _____
5. _____
6. _____
7. _____
8. _____
9. _____
10. _____

Think of your favorite teacher. List 10 words that describe why he or she is your favorite.

1. _____
2. _____
3. _____
4. _____
5. _____
6. _____
7. _____
8. _____
9. _____
10. _____

Same thing, but least favorite teacher.

1. _____
2. _____
3. _____
4. _____
5. _____
6. _____
7. _____
8. _____
9. _____
10. _____

List 10 bad habits. (They don't have to be yours.)

1. _____
2. _____
3. _____
4. _____
5. _____
6. _____
7. _____
8. _____
9. _____
10. _____

List 10 slang words or phrases you and your friends use.

1. _____
2. _____
3. _____
4. _____
5. _____
6. _____
7. _____
8. _____
9. _____
10. _____

List 10 slang words or phrases your parents use. (Embarrassing, isn't it?)

1. _____
2. _____
3. _____
4. _____
5. _____
6. _____
7. _____
8. _____
9. _____
10. _____

List 10 roads in your neighborhood.

1. _____
2. _____
3. _____
4. _____
5. _____
6. _____
7. _____
8. _____
9. _____
10. _____

List 10 really big words you know how to use.

1. _____
2. _____
3. _____
4. _____
5. _____
6. _____
7. _____
8. _____
9. _____
10. _____

If you somehow received a bucket of money, list the first 10 things you'd buy.

1. _____
2. _____
3. _____
4. _____
5. _____
6. _____
7. _____
8. _____
9. _____
10. _____

List 10 places you really want to visit.

1. _____
2. _____
3. _____
4. _____
5. _____
6. _____
7. _____
8. _____
9. _____
10. _____

List 10 words that have the letters "ll" somewhere in them. Like, "smell."

1. _____
2. _____
3. _____
4. _____
5. _____
6. _____
7. _____
8. _____
9. _____
10. _____

List 10 bodies of water.

1. _____
2. _____
3. _____
4. _____
5. _____
6. _____
7. _____
8. _____
9. _____
10. _____

List 10 good friends.

1. _____
2. _____
3. _____
4. _____
5. _____
6. _____
7. _____
8. _____
9. _____
10. _____

List the 10 best songs on the radio right now.

1. _____
2. _____
3. _____
4. _____
5. _____
6. _____
7. _____
8. _____
9. _____
10. _____

List 10 things that sting.

1. _____
2. _____
3. _____
4. _____
5. _____
6. _____
7. _____
8. _____
9. _____
10. _____

List the 10 absolute worst toothpaste flavors you can think of.

1. _____
2. _____
3. _____
4. _____
5. _____
6. _____
7. _____
8. _____
9. _____
10. _____

List 10 catalog clothing colors. For example, instead of "white," you could write, "frost" or "seaweed" instead of green.

1. _____
2. _____
3. _____
4. _____
5. _____
6. _____
7. _____
8. _____
9. _____
10. _____

List 10 things that are "in style" right now.

1. _____
2. _____
3. _____
4. _____
5. _____
6. _____
7. _____
8. _____
9. _____
10. _____

List 10 foreign countries.

1. _____
2. _____
3. _____
4. _____
5. _____
6. _____
7. _____
8. _____
9. _____
10. _____

List 10 other lists you would like to make.

1. _____
2. _____
3. _____
4. _____
5. _____
6. _____
7. _____
8. _____
9. _____
10. _____

Lightning Strikes...

...somewhere on Earth 100 times per second, but what is it?
Lightning is an atmospheric discharge of electricity!

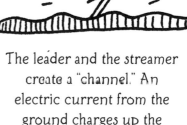

Here's how it works:

The bottom of a cloud carries a negative charge. Below the cloud, positive charges collect on the ground.

The cloud sends down a negative charge, called a "leader." The ground sends up a positive charge called a "streamer."

The leader and the streamer create a "channel." An electric current from the ground charges up the channel and BAM! Lightning!

Since sound travels more slowly than light, you hear the thunder after the flash of lightning.

Create your own perfect storm, with lots of lightning.

The Famous Flying Wedgie...and Others

Fold 'em and fly 'em!

The Famous Flying Wedgie

Step 1: Fold the paper vertically (lengthwise). Crease the fold and unfold.

Step 2: Fold the top corners into the center crease.

Step 3: Fold the triangular top down.

Step 4: Fold the upper corners down. The corners should meet on the crease line.

Step 5: Fold the airplane.

Step 6: Fold the top edges down.

Step 7: Staple the bottom if you wish. Then, place a small paper clip just below the nose.

If the plane dives, bend the back of the wings up a little bit.

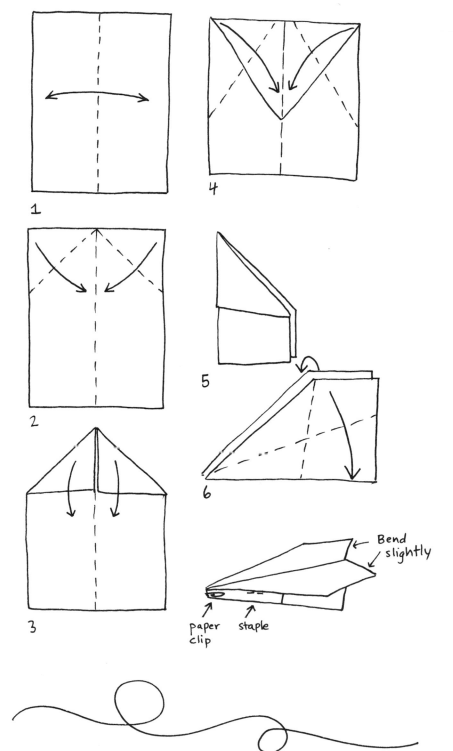

The Spoiler

Step 1: Fold the paper vertically (lengthwise). Crease the fold and unfold. Fold the top corners to the crease.

Step 2: Follow the fold lines in the second illustration.

Step 3: Fold the tip to the inside fold. Crease and unfold.

Step 4: Flip the plane over and fold back over the crease you made in Step 3. Crease and DON'T unfold.

Step 5: Fold the outer sides into the center crease. Crease and unfold.

Step 6: Fold the outer sides back.

Step 7: Fold the wings down. Staple the bottom of the plane if you wish.

Step 8: With the wings still folded down, fold the corners (see illustration)

Step 9: Unfold the wings a little, and unfold the little tabs you just folded (the spoilers).

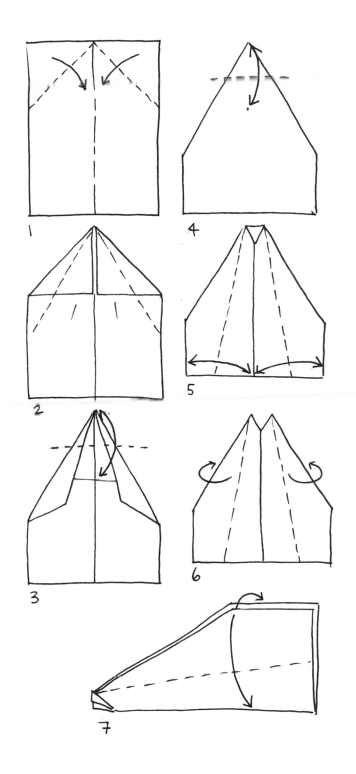

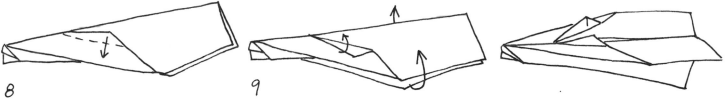

Flying Wing

Step 1: Lay the paper down lengthwise. Fold in half, crease, and unfold. Fold the corners down to the crease.

Step 2: Fold the top point to the bottom edge. Crease and unfold.

Step 3: Fold the tip down to the crease line you made in step 2.

Step 4: Fold the top to the same crease.

Step 5: Fold the top again to where the corners you made in step 1 end..

Step 6: Fold the plane back over itself.

Step 7: Fold the wings down as shown in the illustration.

Try adding a small paper clip to the nose of your plane. Do some experimenting with slight bending of the wings.

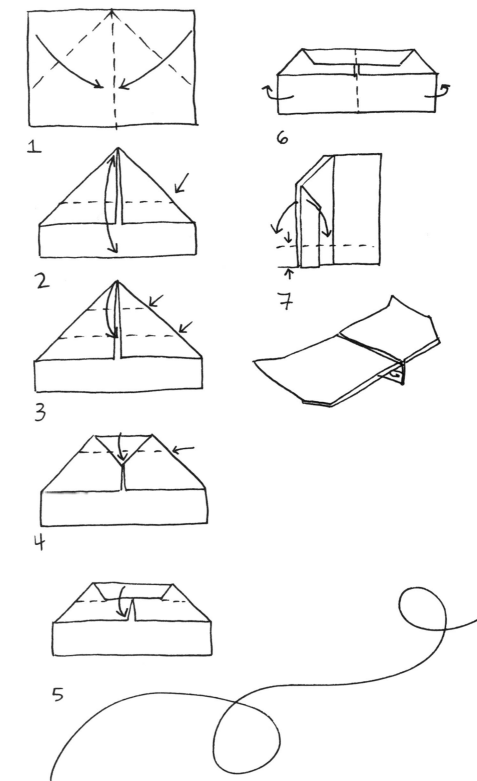

Tag-Team Writing

Who says great authors have to work alone? Pick one of the ideas on this page, then use the next few pages to write a story. Here's the catch—you have to get help writing it. Start by writing the idea at the top of the paper and add your own next sentence. Then, give it to someone else to write the next sentence, but before you give it to them, use a piece of scrap paper to cover all the writing except for the idea and the last sentence written. (You can do this with just one person or a lot of people.) When you get to the last line, uncover the paper and see what bizarre tale unfolds.

Big Ideas

When I came home from school today, I noticed my dog was not in my yard, but instead there was a family of _____. (Fill in the blank.)

Flying looks a lot harder than it actually is.

I woke up this morning with no hair on my head, but a lot of hair growing out of my ears.

I never imagined having to eat bugs, but it happened today.

My team was counting on me to win the game, but they didn't know I had never played before.

Once I decided to ride my bike across the country, things got complicated.

I can't believe my parents replaced the bathtub with a _____. (Fill in the blank.)

My friend had a crazy idea for her pool party—filling the pool with Jell-o.

When I walked outside to get the mail today, the mailbox was glowing neon green.

I bought a bag of candy, but when I opened it, instead I found _____. (Fill in the blank.)

I had a crazy dream that I invented an amazing new _____. (Fill in the blank.)

My family decided to stop driving cars, and ride only horses instead.

Seven Secret Symbols

Stump your friends with this pattern-making game. You're going to make a secret pattern using these seven symbols, and your friend is going to try and guess what it is.

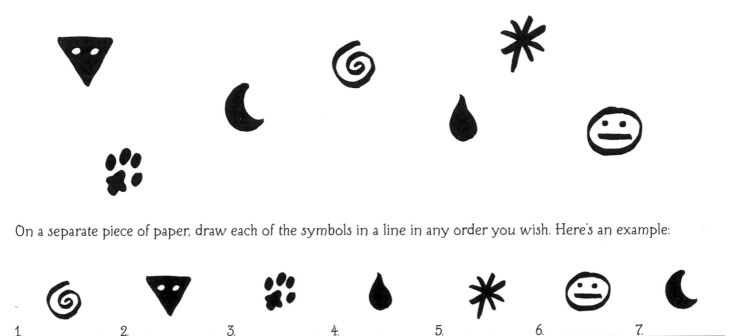

On a separate piece of paper, draw each of the symbols in a line in any order you wish. Here's an example:

1._____   2._____   3._____   4._____   5._____   6._____   7._____

Make sure to use each symbol only once, and don't show your opponent the symbols. Now, your opponent should also write the symbols in any order on the top line on the opposite page. Keep this page available so your opponent remembers all the symbols. Look at your opponent's paper. If any of the symbols are in the same spaces yours are in, circle them. For example, if you and your opponent both drew triangles in space #7, circle the triangle on his paper. He will draw the triangle in this space for the rest of the game.

Your opponent should keep drawing symbols, changing the order for all but the ones that are circled, until all seven symbols are drawn in the correct space, or until the 15 lines are taken up. If the 15 lines are used up before all of the symbols match the order of the ones in your drawing, you win. If your opponent guesses the order in 15 guesses or less, he wins. Play again using the blank paper at the back of this book.

1. _____ _____ _____ _____ _____ _____ _____

2. _____ _____ _____ _____ _____ _____ _____

3. _____ _____ _____ _____ _____ _____ _____

4. _____ _____ _____ _____ _____ _____ _____

5. _____ _____ _____ _____ _____ _____ _____

6. _____ _____ _____ _____ _____ _____ _____

7. _____ _____ _____ _____ _____ _____ _____

8. _____ _____ _____ _____ _____ _____ _____

9. _____ _____ _____ _____ _____ _____ _____

10. _____ _____ _____ _____ _____ _____ _____

11. _____ _____ _____ _____ _____ _____ _____

12. _____ _____ _____ _____ _____ _____ _____

13. _____ _____ _____ _____ _____ _____ _____

14. _____ _____ _____ _____ _____ _____ _____

15. _____ _____ _____ _____ _____ _____ _____

Block City

Draw a big, elaborate block city.

Terrific Titles

Fill in the book spines and covers with titles of books you would want to read.

Terrible Titles

Fill in these book covers and spines with really bad titles.

The History of Three-Pronged Forks

Why? Because, That's Why!

This game is a little bit 20 questions, and a little bit Mad Libs. Below are—you guessed it—20 questions. But you don't really want the answers to them. What you want to do is ask a friend to give you 20 random answers that start with the word "because." Write them down as your friend says them. Then, read back each question and its (undoubtedly) hilarious, mismatched answer. If you don't want to share, you can write down 20 answers yourself without looking at the questions first. No peeking.

1. Q. Why is the sky blue?
    A. Because _____

2. Q. Why do dogs chase cats?
    A. Because _____

3. Q. Why is _____ (fill it in) such a great song?
    A. Because _____

4. Q. Why do my parents make me take long car trips with them?
    A. Because _____

5. Q. Why are most balls round?
    A. Because _____

6. Q. Why is there no school on Saturdays?
    A. Because _____

7. Q. Why is _____ the best sport ever?
    A. Because _____

8. Q. Why does food that is good for us not taste nearly as good as food that is bad for us?
    A. Because _____

9. Q. Why do people climb to the top of a mountain to find the meaning of life?
    A. Because _____

10. Q. Why do some people talk too much?

A. Because _____

11. Q. Why is pizza just so good?

A. Because _____

12. Q. Why do we have Daylight Savings Time?

A. Because _____

13. Q. Why are cell phones getting so tiny?

A. Because _____

14. Q. Why do we have traffic jams?

A. Because _____

15. Q. Why do we get hiccups?

A. Because _____

16. Q. Why do they make cul-de-sacs?

A. Because _____

17. Q. Why do rotten eggs float?

A. Because _____

18. Q. Why do people spit out gum where other people are sure to step on it?

A. Because _____

19. Q. Why do snails move so slowly?

A. Because _____

20. Q. Why do belly buttons make lint?

A. Because _____

The Power of Paper

Here are some pretty cool things you can do with paper.

Cut here for Möbius strip.

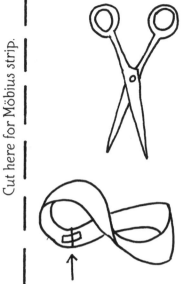

Möbius Strip

This is pretty easy to make and it's...well, it's weird. Cut a strip off of a sheet of paper. (Or, cut along the dotted line on the left.) It should be about 1 inch wide and 10 inches long. Lay the paper flat on the table and twist it one half turn. Then tape the two ends together. You have created an object that has only one side! That doesn't sound like a big deal until you think about it a little. Can you think of anything else that has only one side?

Impossible, you say? After all, that piece of paper had two sides when you started! Try this experiment. Start at the tape on one side, and draw a line down the center of the strip, longways. Keep going until you reach the tape again. The line you are drawing will be on the OTHER side. You have to go all the way around again to get back to the starting point. To really mess with your mind, predict what you think will happen if you cut the strip longways in half. Then, cut a small slit in the strip on the line you drew. Put your scissors through the slit and cut all the way around. What happens? Is it what you expected?

The Big Walk-Through

Start this trick by saying, "Hey, I can cut a hole in this piece of paper and put it over my head all the way down to my feet." Your friends won't believe you, but you can prove them wrong. Take a sheet of paper and cut it along the same lines as the ones on this diagram—place the paper over the diagram and see if you can trace the cut lines. Unfold the cut paper carefully, and put it over your head.

Something in Common

Check out these lists of words. They all have something in common. We did the first one so you'd get the idea. Be sure to give yourself some time with these. Can't figure it out? See the hints below. Then, see page 250 for answers. For "extra credit," look for the * and see if you can come up with the next word in the series.

1) jumping   frisky   mashing   alike   minty   joking   jelly   almond   single   over   nasty   daily
A. Each word starts with the first letter of each of the months of the year, in order.

2) candle   entry   yellow   water   radish   hassle   edges   scrubbing   gifted   dinky*
A. _____

3) steam   dip   scape   peppy   maker   pat   stand   cops   spot   cane   diver   shoe*
A. _____

4) melons   visit   excess   mushroom   jingle   seedling   untie   natural   (party)
A. _____

5) look   out   door   way   side   kick   off   set   back   fire   man   power   house   hold*
A. _____

6) odor   tree   thumb   false   flower   sentence   salt   elephant   nostril   tulip*
A. _____

7) cloudy   flowery   scowl   pearl   later   spine   drinks   math   work   honey   opens*
A. _____

8) story   marshmallow   tiger   wheel   triangle   frighten   salamander
A. _____

9) relish   olive   yams   grapes   bread   icing   vegetables
A. _____

10) amber   bristle   cottage   drank   eyeball   freezer   glance   history   inches*
A. _____

2. Look at the first and last letter of each word. 3. Something's missing. Maybe its the letter R. 4. Visited our solar system lately? 5. Add these together 6. Count to ten. 7. You dont really need the first and last letters, do you? 8. What day is it? 9. Somewhere over the . . . 10. C'mon. This is an easy one!

111

S.O.S.

The trick here is to save yourself when you spell SOS, either across, down, or diagonally. Put either an "S" or an "O" on one of the grids. Let your friend go next and add another S or O. If you spell SOS, draw a line through it and give yourself a point (tally mark) on line A. Your friend should use line B for making tally marks. If you make more than one at a time, you get more than one point. Here's what this looks like:

Board, starting out

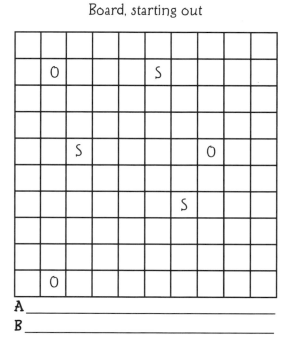

First player's first move

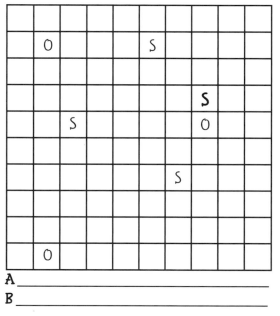

Second player's first move and score

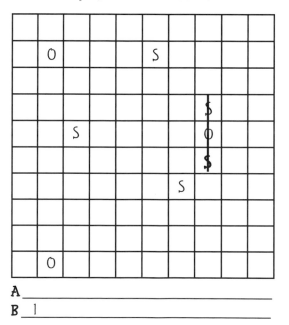

First player's second move and first score

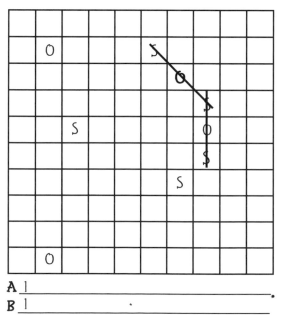

					S				
	O								
		S							
					S				
	O						O		

A ______________________________

B ______________________________

				O	S				
				S	O				
			S						
					O				

A ______________________________

B ______________________________

			S				S		
O									
								O	
					O				
	S								

A ______________________________

B ______________________________

							O		
				O					
				S					
		S							
S	O								

A ______________________________

B ______________________________

A _____
B _____

A _____
B _____

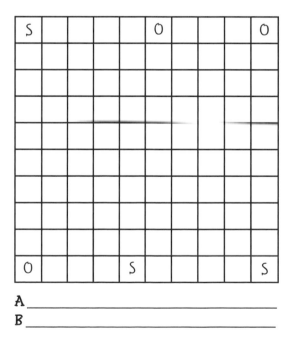

A _____
B _____

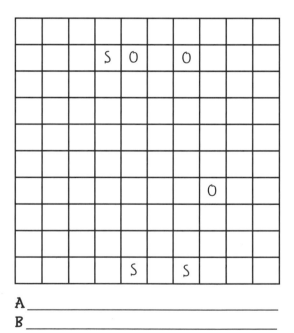

A _____
B _____

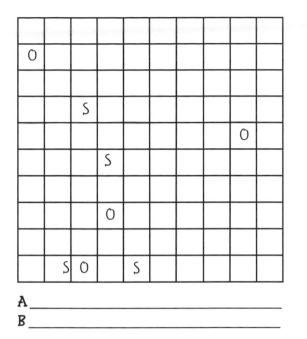

A _____

B _____

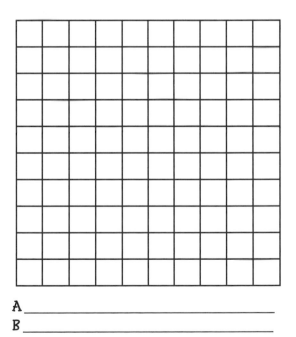

A _____

B _____

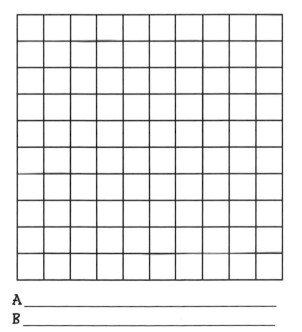

A _____

B _____

A _____

B _____

What's Your Vision?

Everybody in the waiting room failed the eye exam! Please give them all glasses that will match their personalities.

E

F P

T O Z

L P E D

P E C F D

E D F C Z P

D E F P T O C

L E P L C E O

Get Outta Here!

Okay, so most of the time you have your nose in this book, But hey, a little fresh air never hurt. Get outside and play these games.

Roller Bat

Get a bat and a ball of some sort (a tennis ball works well), and go to a place where you won't bust out any windows. Get your friend to pitch the ball and hit it as hard as you can. Hold your arm out and put the end of the bat on the ground. Your friend has to go get the ball, stand where it landed, and throw the ball under your arm between you and the bat. If she can get the ball in, it's her turn to bat. If not, then it's still your turn.

Clothespin Dribble

Basketball isn't all about shooting. It's also about dribbling. For this game you need a friend or two. Each player needs one basketball and three clothespins. First, pinch three clothespins and clip them to the back of a friend's shirt between her shoulders. They should be a couple of inches apart. Do this for all of the players. Then, each of you starts dribbling. You HAVE to dribble the whole time you play this game! When one of you says, "GO," you keep dribbling and try to grab clothespins off of your friends' backs at the same time. If a player stops dribbling or loses all of her clothespins, she is out. Play ends when all but one player has lost all of their clothespins. The person with the most clothespins who is still in the game is the winner.

Pepper

This works better with four or five people playing. One person is the batter. Another player tosses the ball to the batter, who hits it, but not too hard. It's more like a bunt. Everyone tries to field the ball and whoever gets to it first tosses back to the batter, who tries to hit it again. The next player takes a turn hitting when either the batter misses or someone has to run after the ball rather than catch it on a bounce. What's the point? Well, it's fun and it helps you learn to field grounders.

Let's play
H-O-R-S-E

I'd prefer to play
P-I-G

Four Square

To play this game, you need a basketball or kickball and at least four people. Use a piece of chalk to draw a large square, then divide it into four squares. (The four smaller spaces should be about 4 feet square each, and the total size of the square should be about 16 feet.) Number the squares in order, 1–4. The player in space #4 should start by bouncing the ball first in her square, then in someone else's square. That player must bounce it into another square without catching it. Keep the ball bouncing! If a player lets the ball bounce twice, catches the ball, or bounces it out of bounds, that player is out and has to move back to square one while the other players move up. (If more than four players are playing, that player is out while a new player moves into space #1 and the other players move up.) Keep playing until you're tired of it.

Jack of All Blades

Now's your chance to design your Halloween pumpkins without all of that pesky slicing and dicing. Get a marker and make these pumpkins grin and growl.

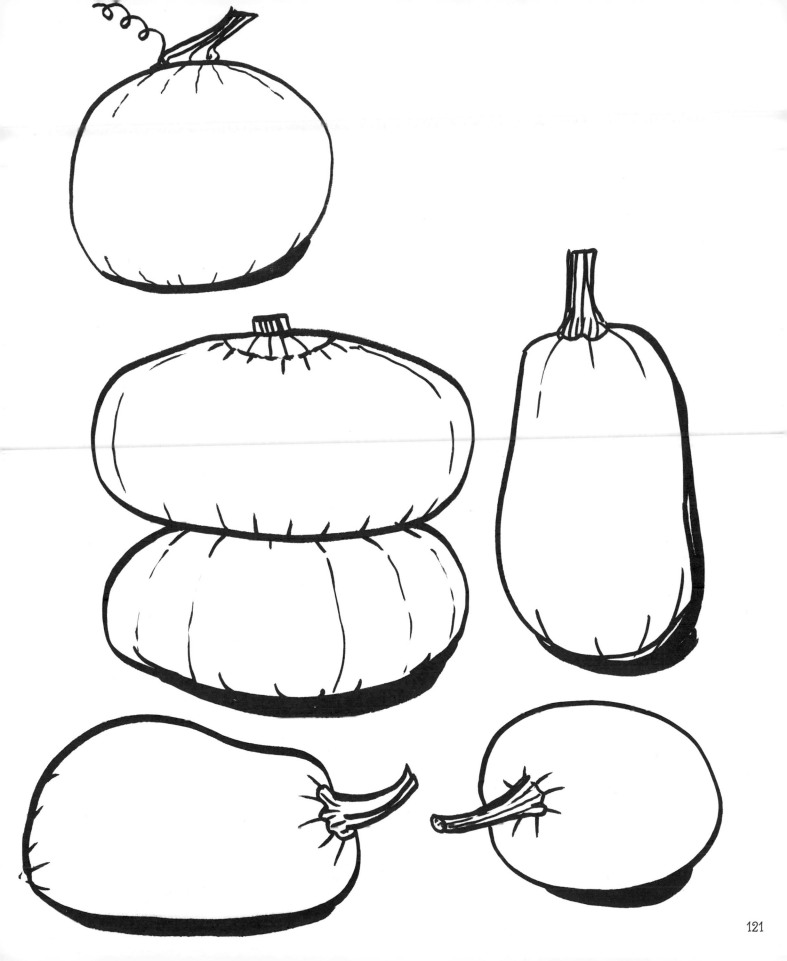

Would You Rather?

Answer these and quiz your friends. You HAVE to choose one of the answers given.

1. Would you rather wear a really ugly, tacky outfit to a party, or walk down the hall at school in your underwear?

2. Would you rather tell a big lie to a friend, or find out that a friend told you a big lie?

3. Would you rather invite everyone you know to a big birthday party, even people you don't like, or just invite two good friends?

4. Would you rather hurt someone's feelings, or get your feelings hurt?

5. Would you rather add a little brother or a little sister to your family?

6. Would you rather do something that scares you and then get over your fear after you did it, or find out that you would never have to do that thing again, but you would always be afraid of it?

7. Would you rather be in charge of a project at school and work with a good team, or work as part of the team with someone who is a really good leader?

8. Would you rather break the hand you write with and be in a cast for two months, or break your leg and be in a cast for four weeks?

9. Would you rather go to school with a huge zit on your nose, or with a visible booger?

10. Would you rather be elected President, or be born to become a king or queen?

11. Would you rather be fun to talk to, or be quiet but always say important things?

12. Would you rather get a shot or have to give someone else a shot?

13. Would you rather never eat your favorite food again, or be able to eat only that food from now on?

14. Would you rather live in a climate with very hot summers and cold, snowy winters, or live where it was always mild and sunny?

15. Would you rather paint every room in your house a different bright, loud color, or paint all of the rooms white?

16. Would you rather cut your own hair or make your own clothes?

17. Would you rather live underwater or on the moon (you could survive in either)?

18. Would you rather stay out late at a great party and get grounded for a month, or miss the party but not get in trouble?

19. Would you rather move to a new school In your city every year, or move only once, but to a city In another state?

20. Would you rather have only a TV, only a laptop, only a cell phone, or only an MP3 player? (You wouldn't have access to the three you did not choose.)

21. Would you rather be very, very good at a sport and get poor grades, or very, very good at academics but be terrible at all sports?

22. Would you rather say something really embarrassing in front of your friends, or make a really embarrassing noise?

23. Would you rather be known to be very kind but serious, or not as kind, but with a great sense of humor?

24. Would you rather swim a mile, run 10 miles, or bike 25 miles?

25. Would you rather answer these questions yourself, or find out your friends' answers?

Tour de _____

(your town here)

You don't have to be from France or named Lance to participate. Chart a bike tour through your town. Draw the tour route and add obstacles, unruly fans, and bikes! Viva the Tour!

Ooooh la la!

Draw Stuff

Add stripes if desired.

Don't forget to add the gobble-ly thing.

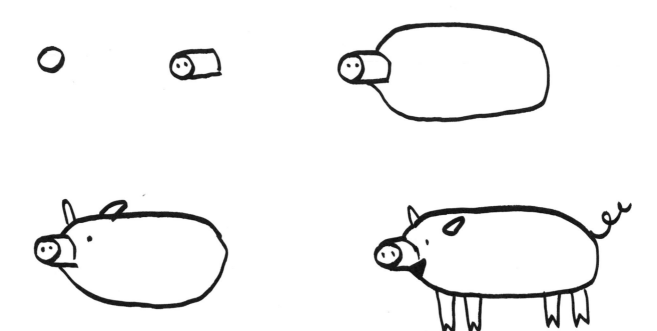

Add an oink here.

Wording Together

This looks like a word search board, but it's really a game you play with another person. Grab a friend and a couple of pens in different colors, and flip a coin to see who goes first. That player gets to circle a word in the board, but not just up, down, or diagonally, like the word "get." Words can be found that way, but they can also be found moving from different rows or columns, as long as you can circle the letters in order without backtracking, as in the word "clipper." Look at the two examples below and you will see what we mean. No word can use letters from another word that is already circled—circles can't overlap. Give yourself a point for each letter in the words you circle—it's easier to keep track as you go. You also get 1 extra point for using a j, q, x, z, k, or v. If you can't find a word, the other player can keep going. When there are no more words, the game is over, and the player with the most points wins.

```
A  C  S  R  X  B  Q  U  E  D  T
F  R  O  A  N  Y  M  B  S  E  R
G  H  T  O  U  K  S  T  P  G  D
E  M  Y  E  I  O  F  D  P  L  Z
T  H  E  H  E  K  B  I  L  C  K
O  I  W  B  Y  G  S  T  J  R  M
P  N  C  D  U  N  C  A  Q  S  E
E  F  L  C  O  G  Z  T  U  A  R
```

```
D E M B U G Z E A W C
F A A Q N I Y I I O O X
Z E O U M R T L A Z I
A B J N A Z U S I M O
R L H E E B N I P E G
T R A C O J A K M U S
L Y A C V I E M E I P
S E L R K R A O D I T
T V O L F G E N P R N
O O W N T R A S A E Y
C W E P E S C Y J O A
```

```
Y A X O K R E E E V N
M C P P O I T J T C H
D O A F L U W T Z L A
A B J N G Z U S I M O
X I Q D E O T R A Z I
O I H B Y G S T J R M
R C S O E M E I E M G
O P S E U Y F N W A R
W G T A Y H K L A T J
A B W I E U C W O D A
F I A D X R O E J O E
```

Memorable Money

Stop! Before you stick that coin into the gum ball machine, take a closer look at it. It could be a commemorative coin. Sometimes, new coins are designed to celebrate special occasions or even remember important people. For example, back in the 1990s, thousands of artists submitted designs to be minted on U.S. quarters that would represent the 50 states. Use the circles below to design your own coins. You can commemorate your school, town, or even your favorite snack.

All in a Name

Maybe your folks finally said you could get a dog (or a cat or a fish or a snake or a Madagascar hissing cockroach). Or, perhaps you have baby brother or sister on the way. Or maybe, you know someday you'll be famous, and you want to make sure you have a name with clout. Use this chart to generate some new names for whatever naming situation you're facing. Choose one boy name and one girl name for each letter.

A _____   A _____
B _____   B _____
C _____   C _____
D _____   D _____
E _____   E _____
F _____   F _____
G _____   G _____
H _____   H _____
I _____   I _____
J _____   J _____
K _____   K _____
L _____   L _____
M _____   M _____
N _____   N _____
O _____   O _____
P _____   P _____
Q _____   Q _____
R _____   R _____
S _____   S _____
T _____   T _____
U _____   U _____
V _____   V _____
W _____   W _____
X _____   X _____
Y _____   Y _____
Z _____   Z _____

Moth or Butterfly?

Both are beautiful winged creatures that hatch from tiny eggs, turn into caterpillars, eat plants, and go through metamorphosis—But what is different about them? Draw moths or butterflies between the wings.

Butterflies
· brightly colored wings
· thin bodies
· active during the day
· antennae have nobs on the ends

Moths
· subdued colors
· thick, hairy-looking bodies
· active at night
· antennae have feather-like appearance

List at Random

Love to make lists? Here are some really random ones.

Think of your favorite school subject. List 10 words that describe why you like it so much.
1. Math
2. Drama
3. Space
4. Gym
5. _____
6. _____
7. _____
8. _____
9. _____
10. _____

Same thing, but least favorite subject.
1. Science
2. S.S.
3. _____
4. _____
5. _____
6. _____
7. _____
8. _____
9. _____
10. _____

List 10 items you can't live without.
1. _____
2. _____
3. _____
4. _____
5. _____
6. _____
7. _____
8. _____
9. _____
10. _____

List 10 things you can do with a piece of paper.
1. _____
2. _____
3. _____
4. _____
5. _____
6. _____
7. _____
8. _____
9. _____
10. _____

List 10 made-up words. (Use them when talking to friends.)
1. _____
2. _____
3. _____
4. _____
5. _____
6. _____
7. _____
8. _____
9. _____
10. _____

List 10 things you're looking forward to.
1. _____
2. _____
3. _____
4. _____
5. _____
6. _____
7. _____
8. _____
9. _____
10. _____

List 10 jobs you might like to do when you grow up.
1. Sing
2. _____
3. _____
4. _____
5. _____
6. _____
7. _____
8. _____
9. _____
10. _____

List 10 challenges you want to attempt.
1. _____
2. _____
3. _____
4. _____
5. _____
6. _____
7. _____
8. _____
9. _____
10. _____

List 10 really gross things.
1. onions
2. garlic
3. _____
4. _____
5. _____
6. _____
7. _____
8. _____
9. _____
10. _____

List 10 websites you like to visit.
1. _____
2. _____
3. _____
4. _____
5. _____
6. _____
7. _____
8. _____
9. _____
10. _____

List 10 awesome movies.
1. Wreck it Ralph
2. Zootopia
3. _____
4. _____
5. _____
6. _____
7. _____
8. _____
9. _____
10. _____

List 10 things that are triangle-shaped.
1. _____
2. _____
3. _____
4. _____
5. _____
6. _____
7. _____
8. _____
9. _____
10. _____

List 10 subjects that you wish were offered in school.
1. _____
2. _____
3. _____
4. _____
5. _____
6. _____
7. _____
8. _____
9. _____
10. _____

List 10 candy bars.
1. Hershey's C&C
2. Kit Kat
3. OH HENRY
4. Coffe Crisp
5. _____
6. _____
7. _____
8. _____
9. _____
10. _____

List 10 words that sound funny when you say them out loud.
1. _____
2. _____
3. _____
4. _____
5. _____
6. _____
7. _____
8. _____
9. _____
10. _____

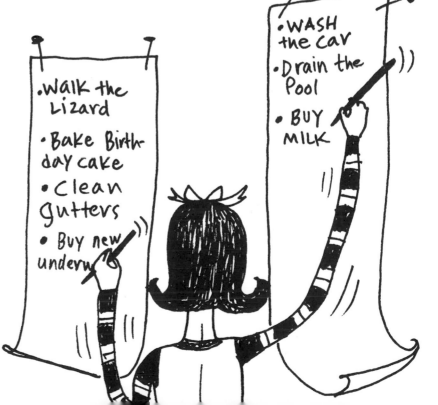

• Walk the Lizard
• Bake Birthday cake
• Clean Gutters
• Buy new underw

• WASH the car
• Drain the Pool
• BUY MILK

Count Your Lucky Charms

On some days, do things just seem to work out exactly the way you want them to? Do you win contests? Do crummy things just seem to happen to other people? Maybe you're just lucky! If not, maybe you need to try one of these lucky charms on for size.

Horseshoes are said to be good luck. Some legends say that since witches are afraid of horses (Why else would they ride brooms?), they are afraid of horseshoes. Other legends say that horseshoes repel fairies because they don't like iron. To have the luckiest horseshoe possible, it's said that you have to find it and not buy it, that it must have been worn and lost by a real horse, and that it helps if the open end is pointed at you when you find it. Then, you have to hang it  "points up" over a doorway where you can touch it as you walk through. (Some do favor the points-down position, so the luck pours all over you.)

Not the nicest of objects, the **rabbit's foot** is a very old good luck charm (except for the rabbits!), possibly dating back to ancient Egypt. Rabbits were considered lucky for many reasons, including that they were a sign of spring and good crops. Another way to use rabbits to invoke luck includes saying "Rabbit rabbit white rabbit" on the first day of each month, or on the New Year, or at the full moon.

Most clovers (shamrocks) have only three leaves,. Finding a **four-leaf clover** is a sign of good luck to come that originated with the Celts and Druids in the British Isles. This is because each leaf stands for something: the first for faith, the second for hope, the third for love, and the fourth for luck, of course! Next time you're near to a patch of clover, sit down and run your hands through it, and have a look. You might get lucky!

Most people hope for a nice, clear wedding day, but some brides and grooms wish for rain. While rain is thought to represent tears from the bride in some cultures, in many others, **wedding-day rain** is viewed as good luck—as a sign of healthy children and bountiful crops ahead. Sometimes companies, especially jewelry stores, make a rainy day lucky for the bride and groom by forgiving the cost of the couple's wedding bands or other stuff.

Speaking of weddings, there's an old saying that tells the bride what to wear for good luck: "**Something old, something new, something borrowed, something blue, and a sixpence in her shoe.**" The something old represents the bride's family and is a link to her past. The new item (often the wedding dress) looks ahead to the future. A borrowed item reminds her that friends and family will still be there for her, and the blue

item means loyalty in the marriage. The sixpence (an English coin no longer in circulation) is supposed to ensure wealth for the married couple. Brides today often follow all of these traditions, sometimes using a different coin besides the sixpence.

Although it's pretty gross when it happens, supposedly it's good luck when a **bird poops on you**, especially on your head. This may be an Italian tradition, or it may be something someone made up after getting pooped on, while everyone else was pointing and laughing.

There are all kinds of legends around the world that describe **seven** as a lucky number. Most of them are based in different religions.

"See a penny, pick it up. All day long you'll have good luck!" The original version of this probably said, "pin." Some claim that pins were used long ago for those who did that sort of thing to cast good luck spells. So finding a pin meant some tangible good luck. A more common thought is—"Hey, free money!" That's almost always lucky, isn't it?

Make a wish on: a falling star, a well, or birthday candles. It's considered good luck to be able to make a wish. People may wish on shooting stars (actually, meteroids— debris found in space that burns up in the Earth's atmosphere) because they are so rare to see. Springs (natural wells) of water were seen in old European traditions as gifts from deities, and therefore had the power to grant wishes. Tossing in a few coins helped ensure that the wishes were granted. Putting candles on birthday cakes may have originated in Greece. Today, many believe that if the birthday boy or girl makes a secret wish and then blows out all of the candles, the wish will come true.

WHAT BRINGS YOU LUCK?

Lucky number _____3_____

Lucky color _Green_

Luckiest day you remember _When i was born_

Lucky item of clothing _____

Unluckiest thing or day you can think of _____
_____
_____
_____

Ever make a wish that came true? What was it and what did you wish on? _____
_____
_____

Do you do anything to bring yourself good luck? _____
_____
_____
_____

Downing the Dog & Lifting the Cat

Feeling burned out? Find a place with a carpet or rug, put on some soft, calm music, and try out some of these yoga poses. Yoga originated in India and has been practiced for over 5,000 years. To do yoga, people combine breathing exercises, physical poses or stances, and sometimes meditation. Today yoga is considered a way to exercise, remain limber, and keep healthy. Often the poses are named after animals. As you try the poses, remember to relax and breathe deeply to get the full benefit, and just do the best you can—don't hurt yourself!

1. The CAT POSE stretches your spine and gets you ready for more yoga. Lower your chest to the floor and put out your arms for PUPPY pose. Relax and breathe! Alternate with the

2. COW POSE for even more stretching and warming up for your spine. Repeat these a few times.

3. From your last COW POSE, move into DOWNWARD-FACING DOG or DOWN DOG for short. This stretches the backs of your legs and makes your shoulders strong.

4. After doing DOWN DOG for several long breaths, stand up slowly and try a hard pose—the EAGLE POSE. You have to balance and concentrate to do this one.

5. Tired from the EAGLE POSE? Lower yourself into DOLPHIN pose. Hold this for a minute, as well.

6. This last pose, the CHILD'S pose, is good to end on. Rest your forehead on the floor and your arms by your sides. Relax. We'll wake you up when something important happens.

Can you make up some of your own poses? Draw them in the boxes below and label them.

Communicart

"It's about so big, and had some things on it, and there was a pointy part on top. Yeah, that's what it looks like." If this sounds like you, maybe you need some practice describing what you see. Give a friend a piece of paper and a pencil, and describe one of the objects below. Tell your friend to draw what you're describing, but don't show them the picture. When you're finished, compare the drawings. If they look different, you need to be more specific, or your friend needs to take out the ear plugs and listen better. If they are the same, either you're a good describer or your friend is a good guesser. If you're taking turns, make sure you cover up the drawings you're not describing.

ColorBlock

This is a great game for spatial people. Play ColorBlock and color yourself a winner!

1 To play ColorBlock, you need a grid (use one of ours) a die (that's half of a pair of dice), two to four players, and a different-colored pencil for each player. (If you run out of grids, no problem. Just use graph paper.)

2 The first player starts by rolling the die. Then, the first player should color in the same number of squares as the number he rolls. For example, if he rolls a 5, he could color five squares. Each square has to touch one of the others along a side (not on a corner).

3 Then, it's the second player's turn to roll and color. The pieces that the second player colors don't have to touch the first player's (although they can). In fact, it helps to spread out as far as possible. That's because if a player rolls a number and can't find enough connected spaces to color that number of squares, he loses his turn. (It helps to roll large numbers at the beginning and small ones at the end, but you have to take what you roll.)

4 Play continues until all players roll and can't find enough squares together to color, or when all the squares are colored. Players should then count their squares. Whoever has the most squares colored is the winner, and gets to go first in the next game.

Perfect Pairs

Salt and pepper, Jack and Jill, night and day—some things are just made to go together. How many perfect pairs can you think of? List them below. To make this a game, have someone else make a separate list at the same time. Spend 10 minutes listing. Then, compare lists and cross out any pairs you have in common. Players can challenge each other's pairs, too. The player with the most pairs at the end (excluding the ones that are crossed out) is the winner.

1. _____
2. _____
3. _____
4. _____
5. _____
6. _____
7. _____
8. _____
9. _____
10. _____
11. _____
12. _____
13. _____
14. _____
15. _____
16. _____
17. _____

18. _____
19. _____
20. _____
21. _____
22. _____
23. _____
24. _____
25. _____
26. _____
27. _____
28. _____
29. _____
30. _____
31. _____
32. _____
33. _____
34. _____

Your friend's score card

1. _____

2. _____

3. _____

4. _____

5. _____

6. _____

7. _____

8. _____

9. _____

10. _____

11. _____

12. _____

13. _____

14. _____

15. _____

16. _____

17. _____

18. _____

19. _____

20. _____

21. _____

22. _____

23. _____

24. _____

25. _____

26. _____

27. _____

28. _____

29. _____

30. _____

31. _____

32. _____

33. _____

34. _____

Just Passing Through

Geese travel in a V shape during migration. Flying in this formation helps the geese save energy, especially for the birds behind the lead goose. Bike racers do the same thing for the same reason, it reduces "drag." Working together, the flock get there faster and with more efficiency.

Honk! Honk!

Goose Facts:
Geese HONK very loudly when they travel.
They are vegetarians.
Males are called ganders.
Baby geese are called goslings.
Females lay between three to eight eggs, called a clutch.
Migration routes are called flyways.

HONK! honk!

Honk! Honk!

Invent your own migrating bird that flies in an "S" or "T" formation here (or any shape you want).
Add ganders and goslings.
Does your bird honk, peep, or shriek?

Slangonyms

Are you a walking thesaurus? Challenge a friend to play Slangonyms. Start by picking one of the words from the top of one of the columns. One of you should write a slang synonym (a word or short phrase that means close to the same thing) on the first line. The other player should write another slang synonym on the next line. Keep going until neither of you can think of another word. The person who writes the last word wins that round. We did a few for you. Notice, they don't have to be current slang!

If you want to change it up a little, play the same game, but with opposite words. Or, don't worry about finding a friend and just make the lists by yourself. For extra laughs, get your parents or grandparents to play. You'll learn some words you'll never want to say in front of your friends.

GOOD	BAD	ATTRACTIVE
nifty		
groovy		
da bomb		

Those shoes are totally funk-a-delic sister-woman!

You should meet my new boyfriend, He's adorkable.

Yo, that concert last night was off the hinges.

Blah Blah Blah Blah Blah Blah

UNATTRACTIVE

_____
_____
_____
_____
_____
_____
_____
_____
_____
_____

BIG

_____
_____
_____
_____
_____
_____
_____
_____
_____
_____

UNCOOL

_____
_____
_____
_____
_____
_____
_____
_____
_____
_____

OLD

_____
_____
_____
_____
_____
_____
_____
_____
_____
_____

FUNNY

_____
_____
_____
_____
_____
_____
_____
_____
_____

ANGRY

_____
_____
_____
_____
_____
_____
_____
_____
_____

Watch What Hatches

Draw what you think will hatch from these eggs.

157

List-en to the Music

Listen to any music lately? Make some lists about what you hear.

List the 10 best songs on the radio right now.
1. _____
2. _____
3. _____
4. _____
5. _____
6. _____
7. _____
8. _____
9. _____
10. _____

Without repeating any of those you just listed, list 10 more musical instruments.
1. _____
2. _____
3. _____
4. _____
5. _____
6. _____
7. _____
8. _____
9. _____
10. _____

List 10 songs you have heard on TV. Commercial jingles count, too. Sing them as you write.
1. _____
2. _____
3. _____
4. _____
5. _____
6. _____
7. _____
8. _____
9. _____
10. _____

List 10 genres of music. For example, rap is a genre.
1. _____
2. _____
3. _____
4. _____
5. _____
6. _____
7. _____
8. _____
9. _____
10. _____

List 10 musical artists.
1. _____
2. _____
3. _____
4. _____
5. _____
6. _____
7. _____
8. _____
9. _____
10. _____

List 10 movie musicals.
1. _____
2. _____
3. _____
4. _____
5. _____
6. _____
7. _____
8. _____
9. _____
10. _____

List the 10 musical instruments, in order, you would most like to play.
1. _____
2. _____
3. _____
4. _____
5. _____
6. _____
7. _____
8. _____
9. _____
10. _____

List your 10 favorite songs of all time.
1. _____
2. _____
3. _____
4. _____
5. _____
6. _____
7. _____
8. _____
9. _____
10. _____

List 10 ways to make music without playing an instrument.
1. _____
2. _____
3. _____
4. _____
5. _____
6. _____
7. _____
8. _____
9. _____
10. _____

List 10 songs you sang as a little kid.

1. _____
2. _____
3. _____
4. _____
5. _____
6. _____
7. _____
8. _____
9. _____
10. _____

List 10 songs you really don't like.

1. _____
2. _____
3. _____
4. _____
5. _____
6. _____
7. _____
8. _____
9. _____
10. _____

List 10 titles of songs you would like to write.

1. _____
2. _____
3. _____
4. _____
5. _____
6. _____
7. _____
8. _____
9. _____
10. _____

List 10 movies with memorable theme songs. Make sure you hum them as you write!

1. _____
2. _____
3. _____
4. _____
5. _____
6. _____
7. _____
8. _____
9. _____
10. _____

List 10 musical notes or terms. (Hint: If you can't read music, start with the alphabet for musical notes.)

1. _____
2. _____
3. _____
4. _____
5. _____
6. _____
7. _____
8. _____
9. _____
10. _____

List the last 10 CDs you bought, or songs you downloaded.

1. _____
2. _____
3. _____
4. _____
5. _____
6. _____
7. _____
8. _____
9. _____
10. _____

This Art Rocks

See the climbers? Draw the cliff face they're climbing.

Pipelayer

All you have to do is get to the other side, but it's not that easy! Grab two different colored pencils. One player gets white dots, and the other player gets black. Player 1 with the white dots is trying to connect a "pipeline" from one side to the other, while Player 2 is trying to connect a "pipeline" from top to bottom. You can connect only your dots. As you connect your dots, try to block your opponent at the same time. You don't have to start with a connected dot, but don't cross any lines. The first player to connect the two edges is the winner. Look below for a sample game and on the next page for a finished board. (Remember, you would make all of these moves on one board!) One last hint: You may want to scatter your lines across the board and connect them at the last minute. It helps fool your opponent.

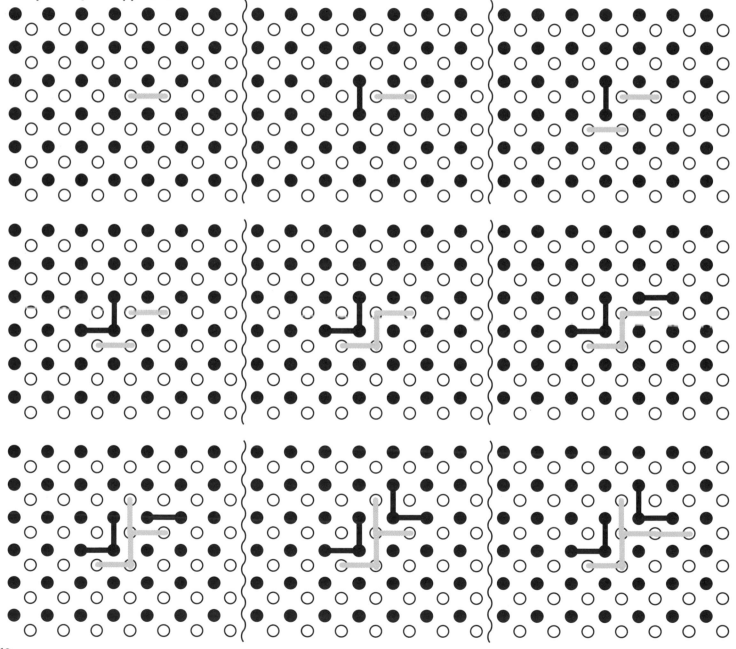

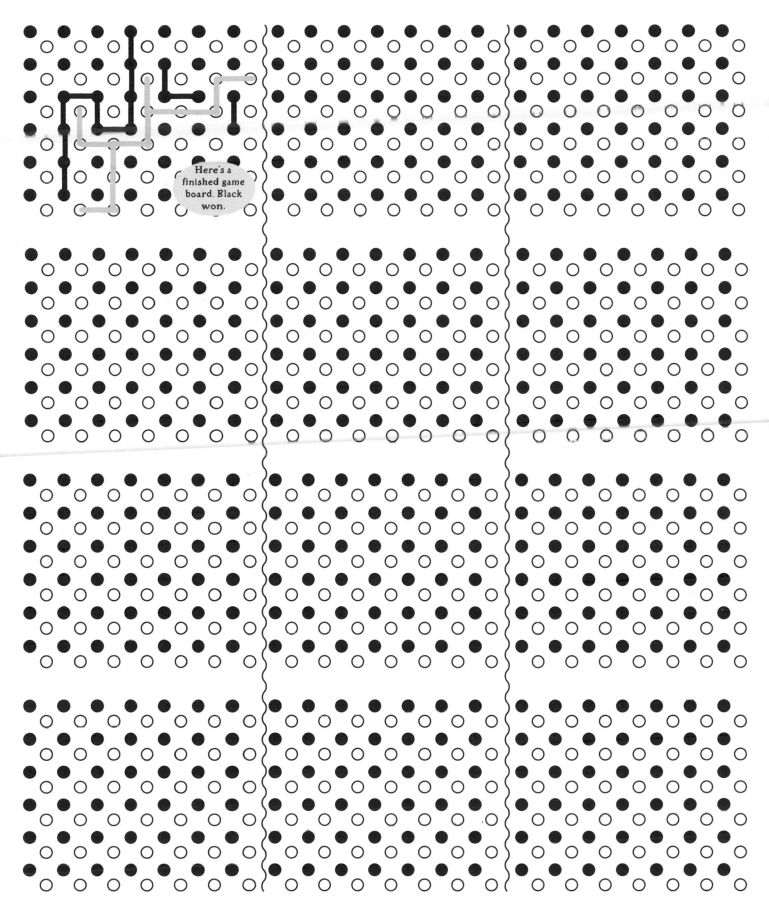

Here's a finished game board. Black won.

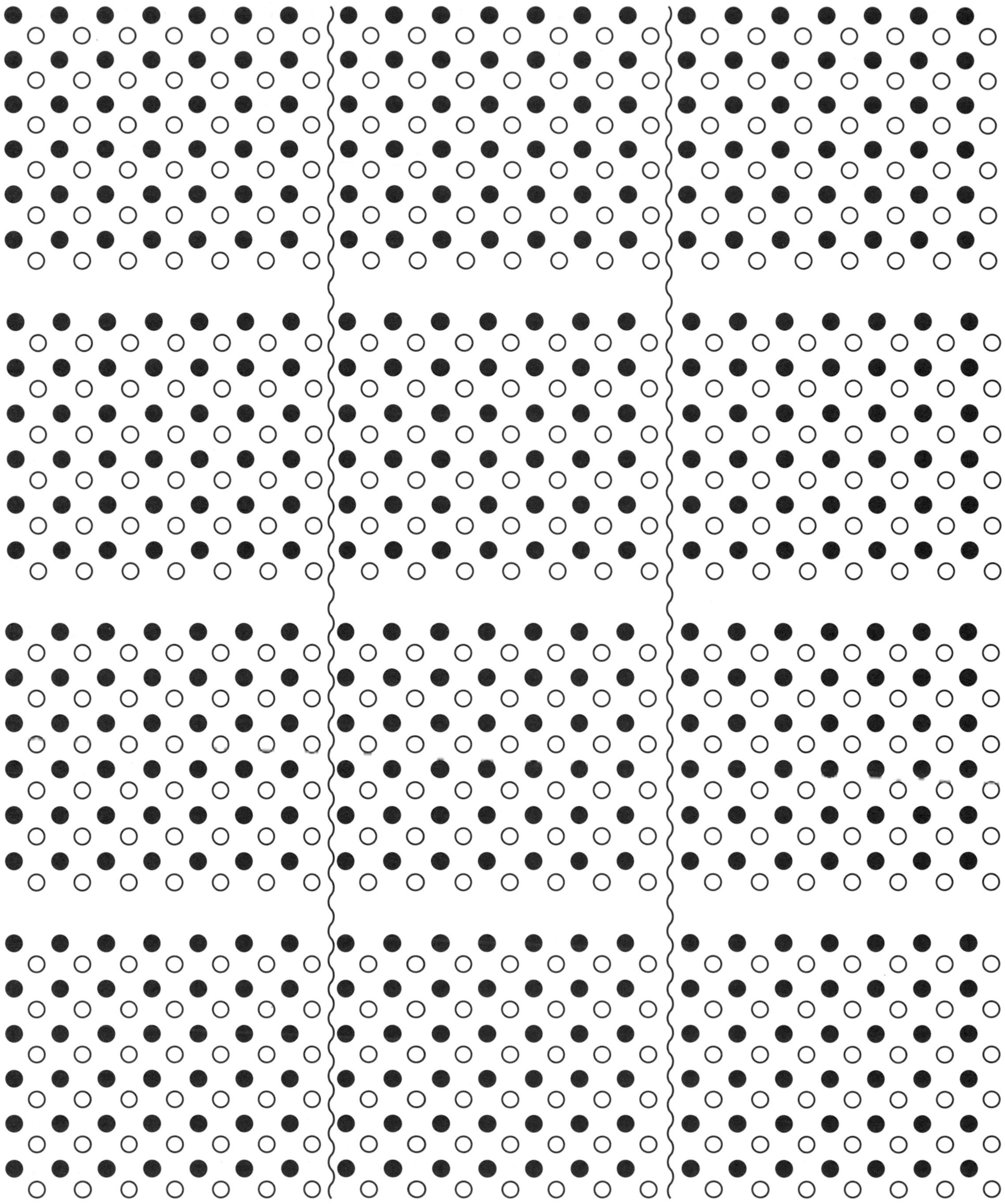

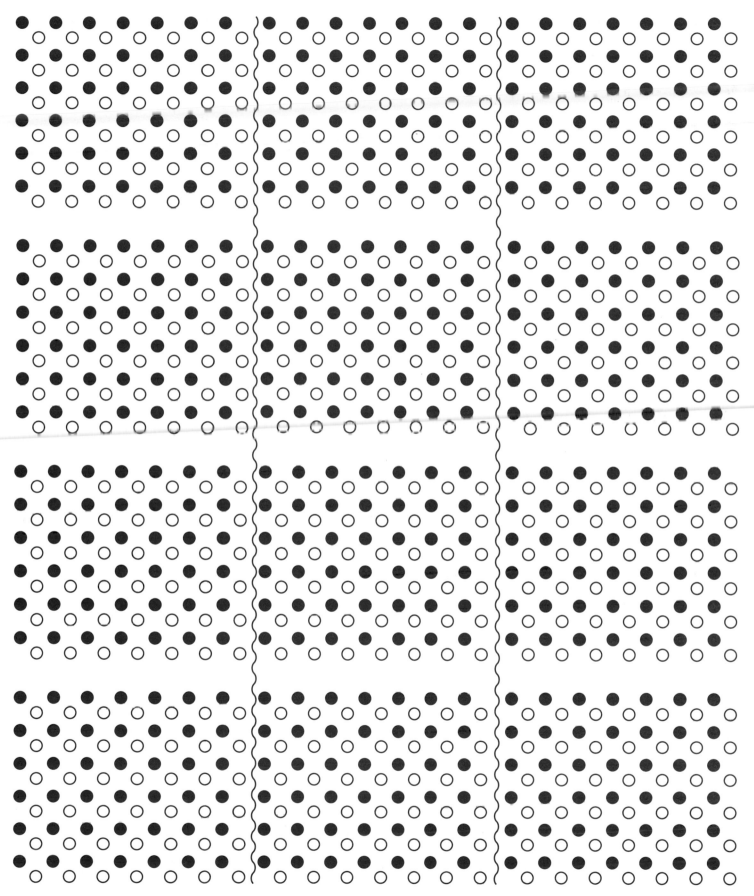

Scary-Go-Round

Who says carousels can only have horses? Draw some amazing creatures!

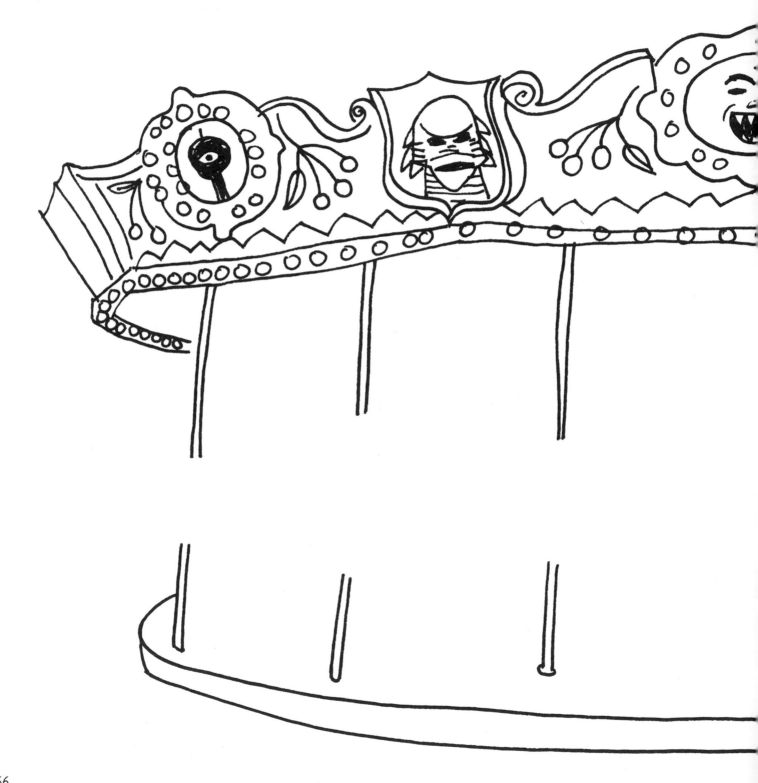

It's a Small World

Draw your own version of the hidden world—germs, viruses, and other tiny, nasty, things.

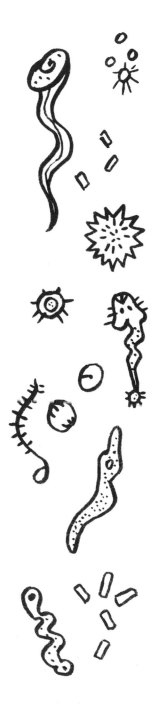

Little Jill neglected to wash for two days. Draw what's all over Jill's hands now.

Alfie's food dish has not been washed in months! What lurks there?

Dylan "lost" his toothbrush for several days. What's living in his mouth now?

Dad's in charge of cleaning the bathroom. (He is very busy.)

What's in a Blob of Ink?

The Rorschach ink blot test is a famous psychological test. People who take the test have to look at 10 inkblots and describe what images they see. Some people think the test works really well, while some people don't think the tests are effective. What do you think?

These aren't the same inkblots used in the test, but it should still be interesting to see what you and your friends think they look like! Show five different friends (including yourself) the ink blots and ask what they see.

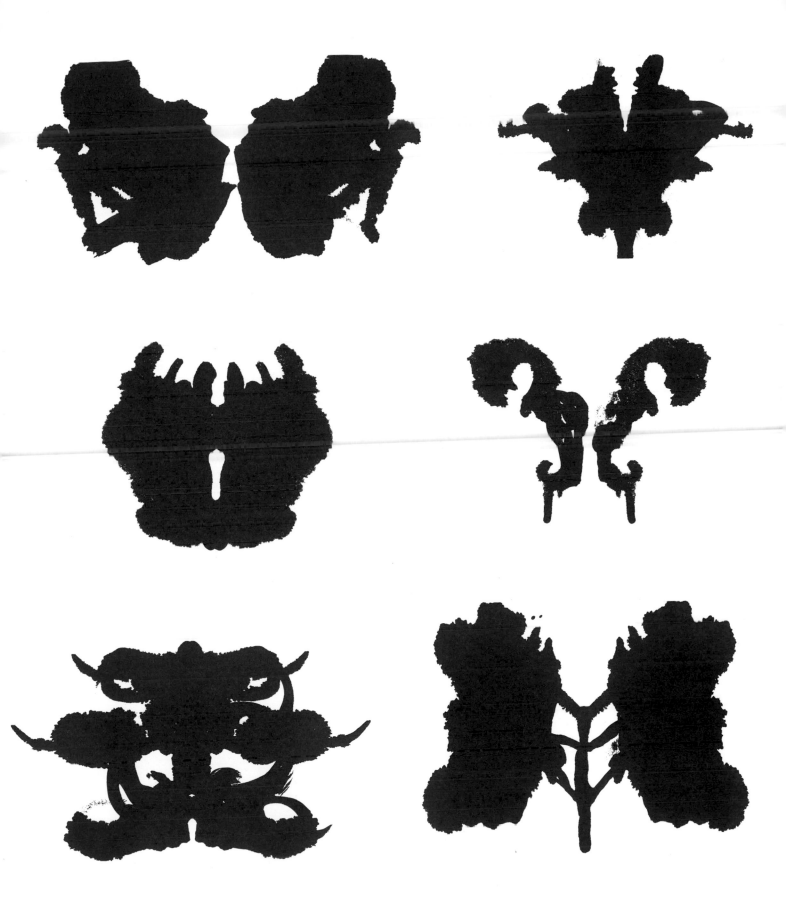

171

Masks

Masks are not just for Halloween. They're used throughout the world in plays and operas, hunting rituals, and even funerals. Design and decorate your own mask, or use the ones provided.

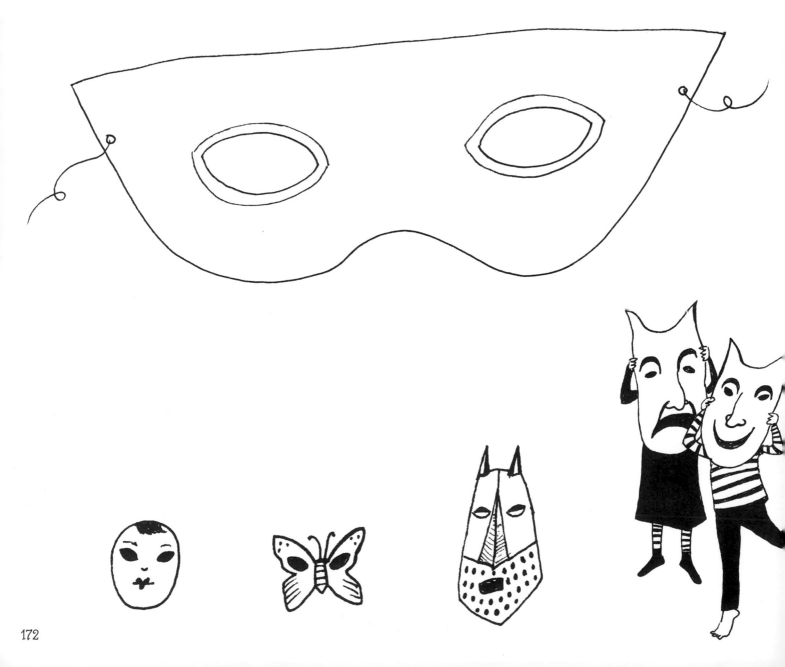

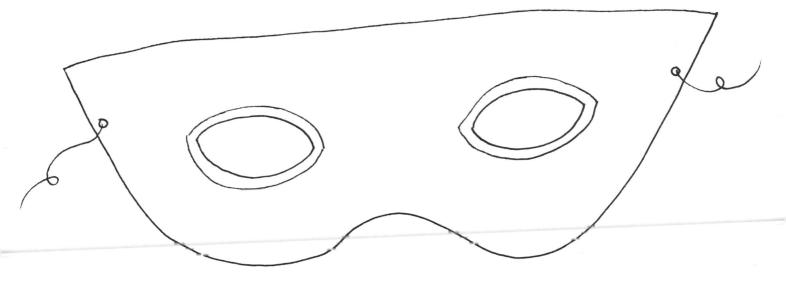

The Eighth Day...

Sunday	Monday	Tuesday	Wednesday	Thursday	Friday	Saturday

The names of the days of the week, as well as the months of the year, were inspired by things like planets, gods and goddesses, political figures, and even numbers. Sunday and Monday were named to honor the sun and moon. Tuesday honored Tiw, a god of war. Wednesday was named for Woden, a god who desired great wisdom. Thursday was named for Thor, the god of Thunder. Friday was named for Frigga, the goddess of nature and marriage. Saturday (along with the planet Saturn) was named to honor the god Saturn, who was thought to control the weather.

People in ancient times were still figuring out how the calendar was going to work. They added days and months to make sure the calendar they followed matched the lunar and solar calendars. Imagine what would happen if we discovered that we needed an eighth day of the week, and YOU were asked to figure out what that day would be! Answer the questions below to decide what you would choose for the eighth day.

Draw a picture of the inspiration for your new day of the week.

1. Think of someone or something you would like to honor. Write their name here. _____
_____

2. How would you change the name to make it match the other day names? _____
_____

3. When would this day be? Between Tuesday and Wednesday? After Sunday? Label the calender strip to show where it would fall.

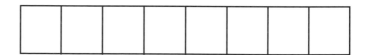

4. What would we do on this day? Is it another work day? A day of rest? How does it measure up to what we do on the other days? _____
_____
_____

& the Thirteenth Month

January february march april may June july August Sept. Oct. Nov. Dec.

The months of the year were named in a similar fashion. January was named for Janus, a god with two faces: one looking to the past and the other looking to the future. It was one of the last two months to be added to the calendar, along with February, which means to "make clean." March was named for Mars, the god of war. April was named for the Latin word "aperio" which means "open up," like blooming flowers. May was named for the goddess Maia, who was thought to protect growing plants. Juno, the queen of Roman goddesses, inspired the name of June. July was named after Roman emperor Julius Caesar, while August was named for his son, the emperor Caesar Augustus. September, October, November, and December were named after the Latin words for seven, eight, nine, and ten, because before January and February were added to the calendar, they were the seventh, eighth, ninth, and tenth months.

1. Make a new month of the year. Think of someone or something you would like to honor. Write their name here. _____

2. Draw your month on this calendar. There are EIGHT days of the week, so be sure to include your new day! Don't forget to add holidays and special days.

Name of Month _____

Season: _____

Last month: _____

Next month: _____

Special holidays: _____

Average high temperature: _____

Average low temperature: _____

Average days of sun: _____

Average days of rain: _____

Average days of snow: _____

Imaginary Friend

Wouldn't it be cool if a new friend moved next door to you? You can't pick your neighbors, but you can pick your friends. Think about what you want in a new friend. Here are some ideas to help you.

Does your new friend
- ☑ Tell really funny jokes?
- ☑ Laugh at all of your jokes?
- ❑ Cry a lot?

Does your new friend
- ☑ Play any sports? Which ones?
- ☑ Like to study?
- ❑ Like to ride the school bus?

Does your new friend
- ☑ Like everything you like?
- ☑ Like different things?
- ❑ Not like much of anything?

Does your new friend
- ☑ Speak different languages? Which ones? _all_
- ❑ Speak only the language you speak?
- ❑ Speak Martian?

Does your new friend
- ❑ Have older brothers and sisters?
- ❑ Have younger brothers and sisters?
- ☑ Have no brothers and sisters?
- ❑ Have a dog?

Does your friend like to
- ☑ Dance?
- ☑ Sing?
- ❑ Go to scouts?
- ☑ Draw pictures or paint?
- ☑ Play an instrument? Which one? _guitar_
- ❑ Play in the mud?

What funny things does your friend do?
- ☑ Drink out of the milk carton when no one's looking.
- ☑ Sneak up on people to scare them.
- ☑ Make faces or do funny impressions of people.
- ☑ Wear crazy hairstyles.
- ☑ Other _make me laugh_
- ❑ My friend is very serious.

What does your friend wear?
- ❑ Crazy striped shirts
- ❑ Lots of black
- ❑ Socks that don't match
- ☑ Hats
- ❑ Glasses
- ❑ Braces
- ☑ Lots of jewelry
- ❑ Polka-dotted underwear

What disgusting things does your friend do?
- ☑ Burp
- ❑ Peel scabs
- ❑ Pick his or her nose
- ☑ Bite fingernails
- ❑ Other _____
- ❑ Nothing; I don't have disgusting friends

What food does your friend like to eat?
- ☑ Pizza
- ☑ Noodles
- ☑ Tacos
- ☑ Burgers
- ☑ Veggies
- ☑ Dessert
- ❑ Dirt
- ❑ Nothing, My friend lives on air.

Now, look back over your answers and draw a picture of your imaginary friend.

How Does Your Garden Grow?

Are you growing flowers or vegetables, or both?

What's growing in the container garden?

Plan your garden here.

What goes here?

Add a bird feeder!

Number Numbers

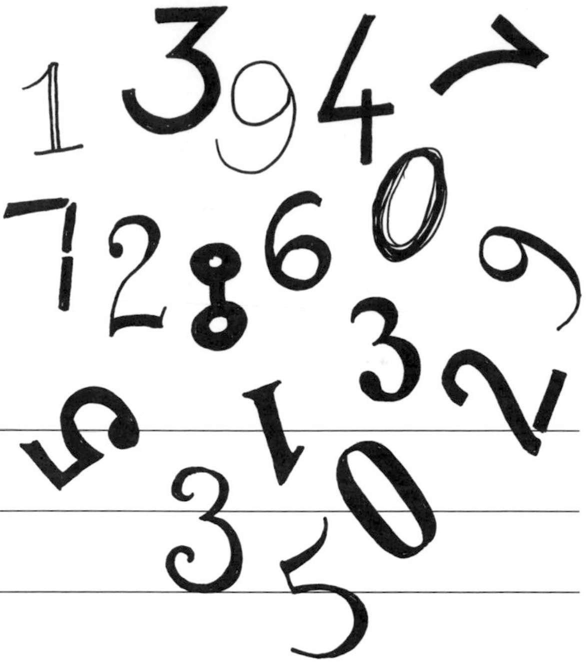

Can you figure out these common phrases?
Use the numbers for clues. Answers are on page 250.

365 D in a Y = 365 days in a year

29 D in F in a LY _____

8 P in our SS _____

5,280 F in a M _____

88 K in a P _____

9 P on a BF _____

3 BM, SHTR _____

7 D in a W _____

52 C in a D _____

26 L in the A _____

12 M in a Y _____

18 H on a GC _____

206 B in the B _____

12 E in a D _____

1000 W that a P is W _____

64 S on a C _____

Pick a Card—a Funny Card

Pick a Card—a Funny Card

If you want to embarrass your friends (and yourself), cut out these cards and put them in a pile. Then take turns picking a card. You HAVE to do whatever the card says, no matter how embarrassing. Ready, set, hide your face!

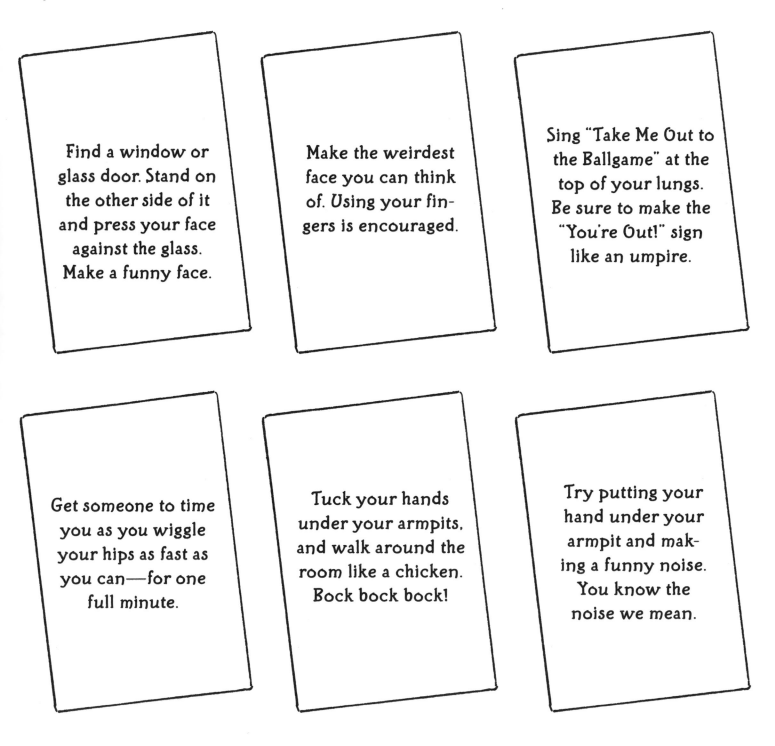

Find a window or glass door. Stand on the other side of it and press your face against the glass. Make a funny face.

Make the weirdest face you can think of. Using your fingers is encouraged.

Sing "Take Me Out to the Ballgame" at the top of your lungs. Be sure to make the "You're Out!" sign like an umpire.

Get someone to time you as you wiggle your hips as fast as you can—for one full minute.

Tuck your hands under your armpits, and walk around the room like a chicken. Bock bock bock!

Try putting your hand under your armpit and making a funny noise. You know the noise we mean.

Do the "robot" dance
for a full minute.
You get to pick out
the music.

Sing the
alphabet song—
like an opera singer.

Do a front roll—a
somersault.

*Use the last two cards to make up your own
embarrassing moments.*

Get Outta Here (part 2)

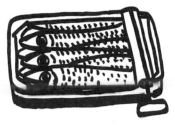

It's time for fresh air again. Get outta here and play some games.

Sardines

This is like hide-and-seek, sort of. You need at least five players for this to be really fun. One person goes to hide while the others count and wait. Then, the waiters split up and try to find the hider. Whoever finds the hider first has to stay there and hide with the first hider. The next person who finds those two has to stay and hide, too. (It helps to stay really quiet while hiding, but it gets really hard since you have to pack into the hiding place like, well, SARDINES. Get it?) The last person to find all of the hiders gets to hide first the next time.

Flashlight Tag

This isn't your little brother's tag. It's all about playing in the dark. You need at least four players, a flashlight, and a place where it will be okay to hide in the dark. (Watch out for things like stairs, ledges, holes in the ground, etc.) Decide on a home base and let one player count to 20 or high enough for everyone to have time to hide. The person who is "it" then has to walk around with the flashlight on the entire time and try to "tag" people by shining it on them and calling out their names before they reach base. The last one to reach base is the next "it."

Spud

This is like horse in basketball. Well, not really, but you spell a word. You needs some open space for this game, unless you like running into things. Get at least five players together and find a big ball like a playground ball or volleyball. One player holds the ball and the others gather around in a circle. The player holding the ball tosses it high into the air and calls out another player's name. Everyone but the person whose name has been called takes off and runs as far as they can. The player whose name was called tries to run in and catch the ball, and when he does, he has to yell, "SPUD!" When they hear the word SPUD, all of the other players freeze. The player with the ball takes two steps toward the closest player and tosses the ball at that player. If the ball hits the player, he gets an "S" (for spud) and is the next person who tosses the ball. When a player gets SPUD, he's out. The winner is the last one to spell SPUD.

Jump the River

The more people you have playing this game, the more fun it is. You need two jump ropes and if you have enough people, a pair of movers. Lay them on the ground about one foot apart (the ropes, not the movers). Line up on one side of the ropes and jump, hop, cartwheel, or whatever over the two ropes, without touching them. After everyone finishes, move the ropes about 6 inches farther apart. Jump over again. Keep moving them farther apart. If someone touches either rope, they're out. As the ropes get farther and farther apart, make sure you leave plenty of room between the ropes and the front of the line so that people can get a running start. The last person to clear the two ropes is the winner.

BookList

Love to read? Forced to read? Make some lists about your reading habits.

List the last 10 book you read.
1. _____
2. _____
3. _____
4. _____
5. _____
6. _____
7. _____
8. _____
9. _____
10. _____

List 10 books you remember reading or having read to you as a little kid.
1. _____
2. _____
3. _____
4. _____
5. _____
6. _____
7. _____
8. _____
9. _____
10. _____

List 10 things to read, other than books. (Yes, lists count!)
1. _____
2. _____
3. _____
4. _____
5. _____
6. _____
7. _____
8. _____
9. _____
10. _____

List 10 of your favorite authors.
1. _____
2. _____
3. _____
4. _____
5. _____
6. _____
7. _____
8. _____
9. _____
10. _____

List 10 books with great pictures.
1. _____
2. _____
3. _____
4. _____
5. _____
6. _____
7. _____
8. _____
9. _____
10. _____

List 10 street signs you remember reading.
1. _____
2. _____
3. _____
4. _____
5. _____
6. _____
7. _____
8. _____
9. _____
10. _____

Check out a bookshelf in your house—yours or someone else's. List 10 books you see.
1. _____
2. _____
3. _____
4. _____
5. _____
6. _____
7. _____
8. _____
9. _____
10. _____

List things you learned from reading.
1. _____
2. _____
3. _____
4. _____
5. _____
6. _____
7. _____
8. _____
9. _____
10. _____

List 10 magazines.
1. _____
2. _____
3. _____
4. _____
5. _____
6. _____
7. _____
8. _____
9. _____
10. _____

Make up 10 weird book titles. List them here.

1. _____
2. _____
3. _____
4. _____
5. _____
6. _____
7. _____
8. _____
9. _____
10. _____

List 10 "bad guy" characters from books you have read.

1. _____
2. _____
3. _____
4. _____
5. _____
6. _____
7. _____
8. _____
9. _____
10. _____

Make up 10 scary book titles. List them here.

1. _____
2. _____
3. _____
4. _____
5. _____
6. _____
7. _____
8. _____
9. _____
10. _____

List 10 most memorable book characters.

1. _____
2. _____
3. _____
4. _____
5. _____
6. _____
7. _____
8. _____
9. _____
10. _____

List 10 self-help or how-to books you'd like to own.

1. _____
2. _____
3. _____
4. _____
5. _____
6. _____
7. _____
8. _____
9. _____
10. _____

List 10 nonfiction things you like to read about.

1. _____
2. _____
3. _____
4. _____
5. _____
6. _____
7. _____
8. _____
9. _____
10. _____

The Ultimate Birthday Cake

We made the cakes, you add the decorations. What will they be? Sprinkles? Mini-candy bars? Confetti? A lot of candles? Fancy icing?

The Code to Rome

The Ancient Romans used combinations of the seven letters on the chart below to make numbers. Roman numerals are much less common these days, but they can be really useful in making a code that's fun to crack. Put on your toga and use the charts and the "rules" to answer the riddles below. Answers on page 251.

Roman Numeral Hints
· I = 1, V = 5, X = 10, L = 50, C = 100, D = 500, M = 1,000
· III = 3 (Up to three numerals of the same value can be shown to be added together.)
· IV = 4 (Putting a smaller number before a larger one shows that the smaller one is subtracted from the larger. This is used for numbers 4, 9, 14, 19, 40, 90, and so on.)
· LI = 51 (Putting a smaller number after a larger one shows that the two numbers are added together.)

The Code (It's very easy, except it will be written in Roman numerals!)

A	B	C	D	E	F	G	H	I	J	K	L	M
1	2	3	4	5	6	7	8	9	10	11	12	13

N	O	P	Q	R	S	T	U	V	W	X	Y	Z
14	15	16	17	18	19	20	21	22	23	24	25	26

Q. How many months have 28 days?
A. I XII XII   XV VI   XX VIII V XIII.

_____

Q. How many birds can you fit into an empty nest?
A. XV XIV V.   I VI XX V XVIII   XX VIII I XX   IX XX   IX XIX XIV · XX
V XIII XVI XX XXV   I XIV XXV XIII XV XVIII V!

_____

Q. How do you make a slow horse fast?
A. XIX XX XV XVI   VI V V IV IX XIV VII   IX XX.

_____

Q. What did the lawyer name his daughter?
A. XIX XXI V.

_____

Match the Roman numerals to their numbers.

1. LXVIII is the same as:
a. 48   b. 55   c. 68   d. 43

3. DXL is the same as:
a. 540   b. 560   c. 640   d. 550

2. MCDXX is the same as
a. 1,240 b. 1,420 c. 1,620 d. 1,622

4. CXCIV is the same as
a. 214   b. 196   c. 194   d. 216

Put these Roman numerals in order.

5.   XIX   XXX   XXXIV   XX   XXIV   VII   XXVII   XXVIII   XXXI   XXV

_____

6.   XL   L   LXII   LV   LXI   LXIV   LIX   LXX   LXXIX   LXV

_____

7.   CL   XC   XCVIII   CI   XCV   CLXIV   CCXC   CCC   CXL   CCL

_____

Write these numbers as Roman numerals.

8. 597 _____   9. 1,437 _____   10. 3,949 _____

Create your own Roman numeral code.

_____

_____

_____

Big Plans

Design the house of your dreams.

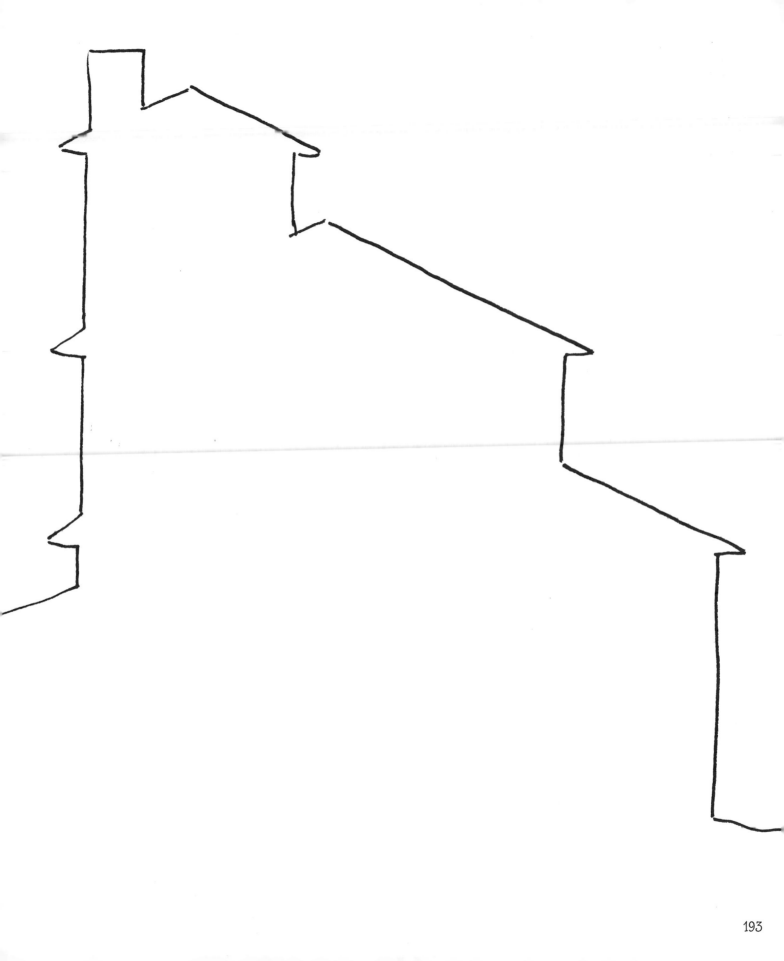

Let's Get Something Straight

Help these folks get straighted out, We mean their teeth.
Add braces, please!

Undersea Garden

A coral reef is made up of brightly colored marine animals that have their skeletons on the outside—called exoskeletons. These animals make a nice home for several sea creatures, including: sea urchin, sponges, jellyfish, sea turtles, and parrot and angelfish.

Draw your own coral reef and the marine life that live there.

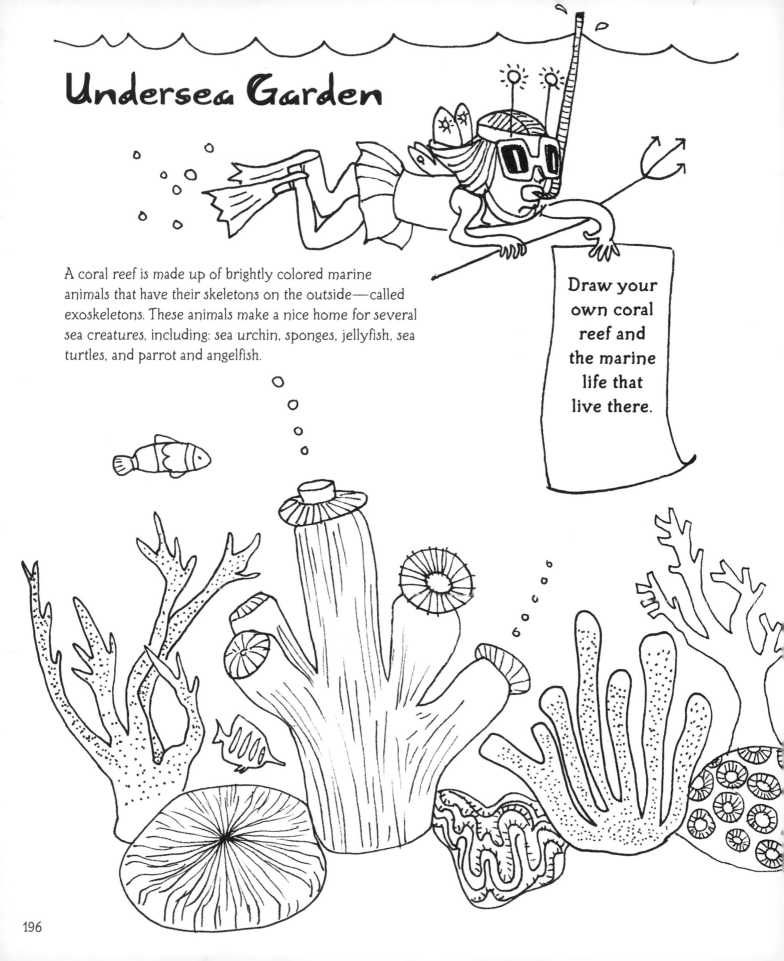

Get out the colored pencils and paints. A healthy coral reef is very colorful!

Wizard Keys

Help this befuddled Wizard find his keys. He can't go anywhere without them. There are 12 keys. See page 251 for the answers.

Tiny Trees

Bonsai is the art of trimming or tying back branches and roots to produce dwarf shrubs and trees from plants that would normally grow to full size. The art form is inspired by plants that grow in rocky areas of Japan and sometimes China. Usually, the plants that are considered the best bonsai specimens are those that look like real trees in miniature—weathered trunks, tiny but well-formed leaves, and partially exposed roots—that are grown to a carefully planned form. The containers are an important part of the art form, too, and should match the trees.

Growing real bonsai often takes many years and lots of skill. You can practice here. Draw some bonsai trees in these containers. Think about how to match the trees to the containers, how to make them look like real trees, and what art form you want to create. Then, you can draw some tiny swings and tree houses, and carve tiny initials into them. Just kidding.

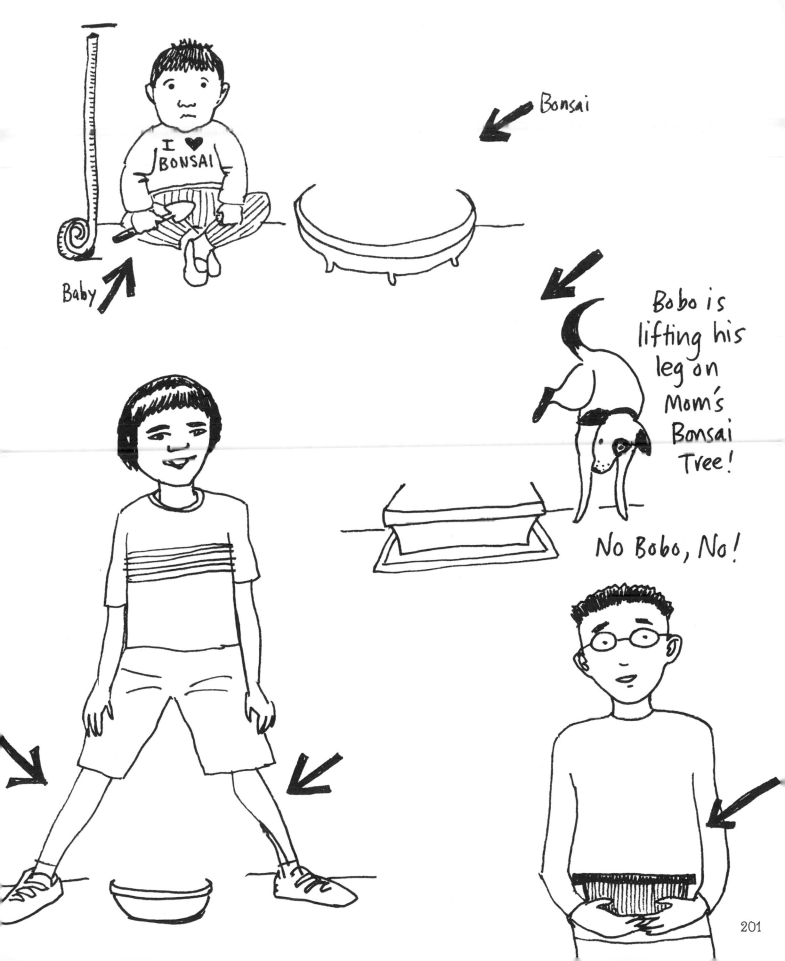

Bonsai

Baby

Bobo is lifting his leg on Mom's Bonsai Tree!

No Bobo, No!

201

Time for Play

You're lucky, because you have just been asked to design a new school playground. You don't have a budget—it can be as elaborate as you like. Below is the drawing space for the initial plan.

Here are guidelines you have to follow in order to conform to some safety rules.

1. Provide a soft area around climbing structures. Be sure to label all kinds of surface areas as you design (grass, concrete, mulch, etc.).
2. Put ample space around bottoms of slides.
3. Swings should be off by themselves and on level ground.
4. There should be a clear field of view to each apparatus so teachers can supervise the kids.
5. Raised surfaces should have guardrails.

Spot the Differences

There are plenty of differences between these two pictures. We think there are about 25, but maybe you can find more. Give it a shot. Answers on page 251.

205

Full of Hot Air

Ever wish you could fly up, up, and away? We have provided the baskets, you provide the balloons. People design hot air balloons with colors and graphics, with flat racing "gores" (the vertical panels around the balloon) or very bumpy ones, with advertisements on them, and sometimes with unusual shapes or appendages.

Don't Say Cheese!

If you've ever seen very old photographs of people (taken in the 1800s and early 1900s), you'll notice that they almost never smile. There are several reasons for all of these serious photos. One is that people had to sit very still for 10 minutes or more, and smiling that long is very difficult. Also, people had to spend quite a bit of money to have their pictures taken, and they took it very seriously.

Fill these frames with pictures of people who don't smile. They can be modern or old-fashioned.

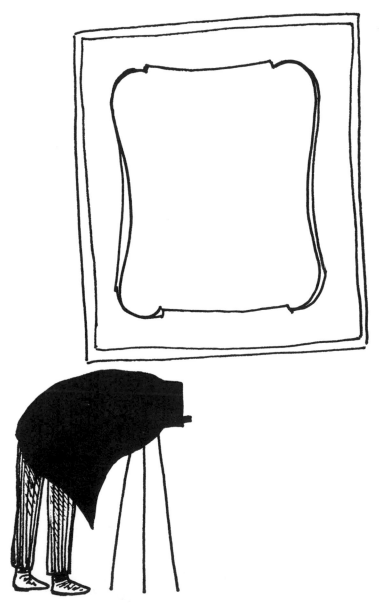

That Kemp Is a Reacher!
(That hot rod is dependable!)

Most of the time, a car is just a car. But sometimes, it's a rod. A hot rod or street rod is a car with changes made to the engine, body, or both, to make it run better and look cool. Design your own.

Use these fun rod words to inspire your art creation.

Balonies: Really wide, rear tires

Beast: An ugly hot rod

Coupe: Any car that has only a front seat

Ghost flames: Flames down the side of the car that are almost the same color as the main paint job

Kemp: A rod with a customized body

Mood disks: Flat aluminum wheel covers

Reacher: A dependable street rod that performs well

Scallop: A painted-on design shaped like a long, skinny triangle that starts at the front of a rod and runs down the side

Zoomy: A crazy-looking street rod with exposed exhaust pipes

And the Winner Is...

Everybody deserves an award for something. Awards can be really nice and still be a little funny. Imagine giving a "Best Baseball Player in the Family" to your brother—who's also the ONLY baseball player in the family. Or giving the "Always on Time No Matter What" award to your mom because she's always made you get up REALLY early for school. Maybe your sister gets the award for "Most Likely to Look Great for School" because she's an enormous bathroom hogger, or your dad should get an award for "Most Popular at Dinner Time" because his cell phone is always ringing just as you're sitting down to eat.

Label these fabulous awards, cut them out, and give them to your friends and family. Remember, the point is to give a little recognition, not to hurt anyone's feelings. If you're brave enough, save a couple for people to give to you.

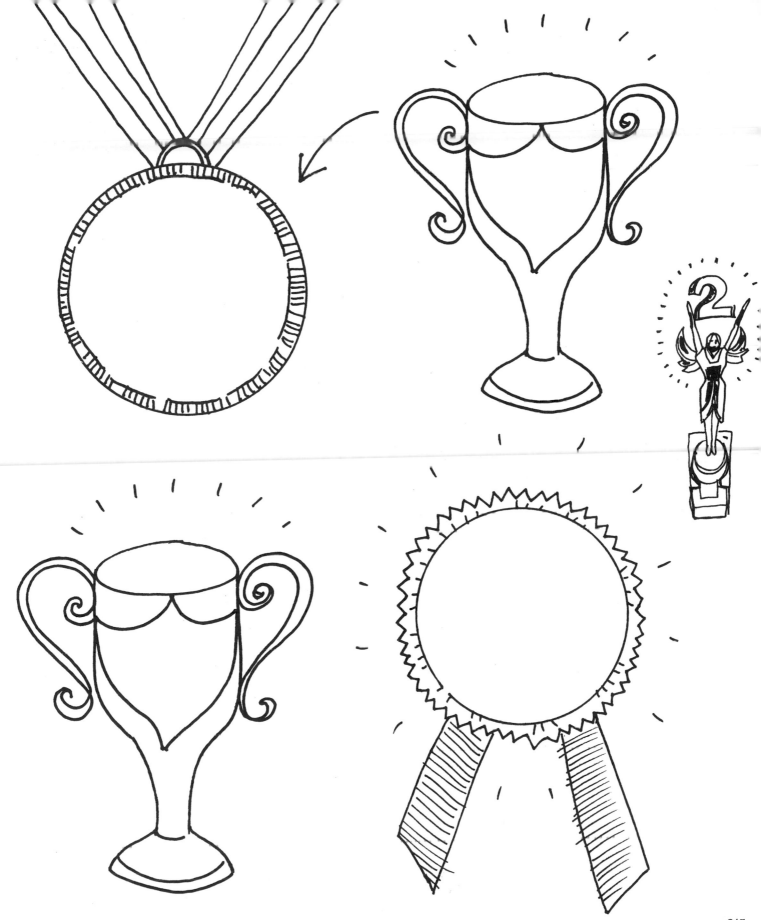

Can I Have Your Autograph?

Even if you don't end up famous, as you get older, you'll be asked more and more to sign your name. You'll have to sign checks, sign for packages, and maybe even sign autographs. Since so many people will be clamoring for your signature, maybe you should practice. Write your name on the lines below. Here are some pointers.

1. First, just sign your name. See what it looks like. Do you like it? What would you like to change about it?

2. Decide what you want to emphasize. Usually, the first few letters are more clear than the last few. Practice here.

3. Want to add some flair? Think about adding something interesting that you don't use in your everyday writing. Do you want to underline your name? Dot your i or cross your t in an exceptional way? Make the first letter of your first name exceptionally large? Pick one or two special things that you only do in your signature. Try a couple of different things to see what looks right to you.

4. Now, practice signing your name quickly. This will come in handy when you have to sign a lot of documents.

Use this page to practice.

Clichés? OK!

These clichés are similes. They compare two very different things using the words "like" or "as." Can you fill in the blanks? Answers on page 252.

Blind as a _____ .
Strong as an _____ .
Snug as a _____ .
Sly like a _____ .

Proud as a _____ .
Clear as a _____ .
Hard as a _____ .
Deep as a _____ .

Dead as a _____ .
Sharp as a _____ .
Thin as a _____ .
Dark as _____ .

White as a _____ .
White as _____ .
Busy as a _____ .
Straight as an _____ .

Light as _____ .
Quiet as a _____ .
Soft as a _____ .
Big as a _____ .

Sick as a _____ .
Flat as a _____ .
Happy as a _____ .
No more—we're as lazy as a daisy.

Triangle

This is a little like checkers in that you can jump over (your own) men, but instead of keeping as many as possible, you're trying to leave just one. Put a small game piece, like a small piece of candy-coated chocolate on every space but one. (You pick which one.) Each time you jump over a game piece with another piece, remove the game piece you jumped over from the board. (There's the advantage of using candy—you can eat the pieces you remove.) Keep jumping until you don't have any more moves—there will either be one game piece left, several left with spaces in between so you can't jump over another game piece to move, or there will be several game pieces that fill a horizontal or vertical row. If you get through half a bag of candy without managing to leave just one on the board, turn to page 252 for one solution. If you manage to finish with the peg in the center hole, you get extra points. How many? Uh, 12. Here's the scoring key.

Leave 5 pegs—Wow. That's really square. (That's an old word that means lame.)
Leave 4 pegs—You're coming around.
Leave 3 pegs—Keep trying—you're getting an angle.
Leave 2 pegs—You're a star!
Leave 1 peg—You have mastered the triangle.

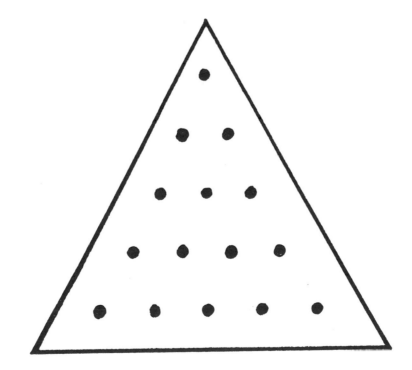

Spot-On

Add spots to these things.

Making Waves

Are these boats having a nice cruise or on the verge of sinking into the ocean? Draw some waves, if that floats your boats. Is there a sea creature lurking under the water? Some treasure? Man overboard?

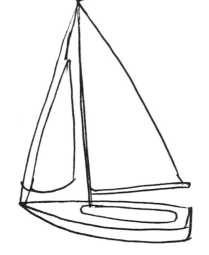

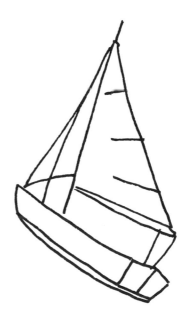

MASH-ing the Future

Did you know you can predict the future? It's easy if you MASH it. Fill out the lists below. Then, draw a spiral, like this, ⊚ in the center box. Don't peek at the next page until you finish your spiral!

M A S H

List five animals.

_____
_____
_____
_____
_____

List seven cities.

_____
_____
_____
_____
_____
_____
_____

List seven careers.

_____
_____
_____
_____
_____
_____
_____

List five people.

_____
_____
_____
_____
_____

List seven cars.

_____
_____
_____
_____
_____
_____
_____

List five small numbers.

_____
_____
_____
_____
_____

List seven colors.

_____
_____
_____
_____
_____
_____
_____

Okay, now count the number of lines in your spiral from top to bottom. For example, the little spiral at the top of the page has six lines from top to bottom. This is now your magic number! Starting with the letter M in MASH, count the rest of that word and your answers until you reach the number of lines in your spiral. Let's say your spiral has six lines. Count like this: M = 1, A = 2, S = 3, H = 4, first car = 5, second car = 6. Draw a line through the last thing you count (in this case, it's the second car), and start counting again on the next answer (the third car, in this case). Keep counting clockwise, marking off answers every time you get to six, until you have just one answer left in each category. As you go around counting your answers, don't count crossed-out entries. See the next page on how to read your answers.

MASH
(FOR A FRIEND)

List five animals.

_____
_____
_____
_____
_____

List seven cars.

_____
_____
_____
_____
_____
_____
_____

List seven cities.

_____
_____
_____
_____
_____
_____
_____

List five small numbers.

_____
_____
_____
_____
_____

List seven careers.

_____
_____
_____
_____

List five people.

_____
_____
_____
_____

List seven colors.

_____
_____
_____
_____

M = mansion, A = apartment, S = shack, H = house: The one that's left is where you will live.
The car and color that are left are the kind and color of car you will drive.
The small number that's left is how many children you will have.
The person that's left is your best friend in the future.
The job that's left is what you will do when you grow up.
The city that's left is where you will live.
The animal that's left is the kind of pet you will keep.

Penny Cricket

This is for those people who like to throw their money around. Cricket is a dart game that originated in England, but here you can play this modified version with three pennies. To make the game board, cut out the two half circles on the following two pages and tape them together. You can either play with one other person, or three other people using teams of two. (When playing with four players, players on the same team alternate turns.)

If you look at the scorecard below, you'll see the numbers 15 through 20 and the letter "B," which stands for "bull's-eye." These are the numbers you use in cricket. Write each player's or team's name on one of the sides of the scorecard.

To play, place the target on the floor. The first player should kneel over the game board and drop the pennies from about a foot up, one at a time. If a penny lands on any of the numbers 15 through 20, put a slash mark (\) on the board. The penny must be more than 50% in the space to get a slash mark. If it's exactly between two numbers, you get the lower score. If the penny lands entirely on the bull's-eye, put a slash mark next to the "B." After three pennies are dropped, it's the next player's turn.

The first player or team to land on each number and the bull's-eye is the winner. For an added challenge, change the rules so that each player or team has to land on each number and bull's-eye three times. Good Luck!

PLAYER 1			PLAYER 2
		20	
		19	
		18	
		17	
		16	
		15	
		B	

Penny Cricket Board

Caption Creation

Make up some headlines for these front-page stories.

Photo-Journalism

Now, make up some photos and headlines for these front-page stories.

Who's Your Friend?

Think you know your friends? Instead of answering these questions for yourself, write the answers that you think a particular friend or family member would give. Then, read the questions out loud to your friend (or your mom or sister or whoever). Meanwhile get your friend to do the same thing to you. Trade answers and see how many you both got right. Give yourself a point for each answer you guessed correctly.

Your Guess   /   Actual Answer

1. Who do you think should be the next leader of your country? _____ / _____

2. What makes you happiest? _____ / _____

3. What are you most afraid of? _____ / _____

4. If you were going to plant something, what would it be and where would you plant it?

_____ / _____

5. What makes you a good friend to other people? _____ / _____

6. What is your favorite game to play? _____ / _____

7. Where would you most like to travel? _____ / _____

8. What color would you like to paint your bedroom? _____ / _____

9. Would you rather ice skate, roller skate, roller blade, or skateboard? _____ / _____

10. What one thing would you most like to change about yourself? _____

_____ / _____

11. Who is your hero? _____ / _____

12. What do you want to do on your next birthday? _____ /

_____

Bubble Bubble

Fill this bathtub—with bubbles, boats, rubber ducks, or anything else that comes to mind.

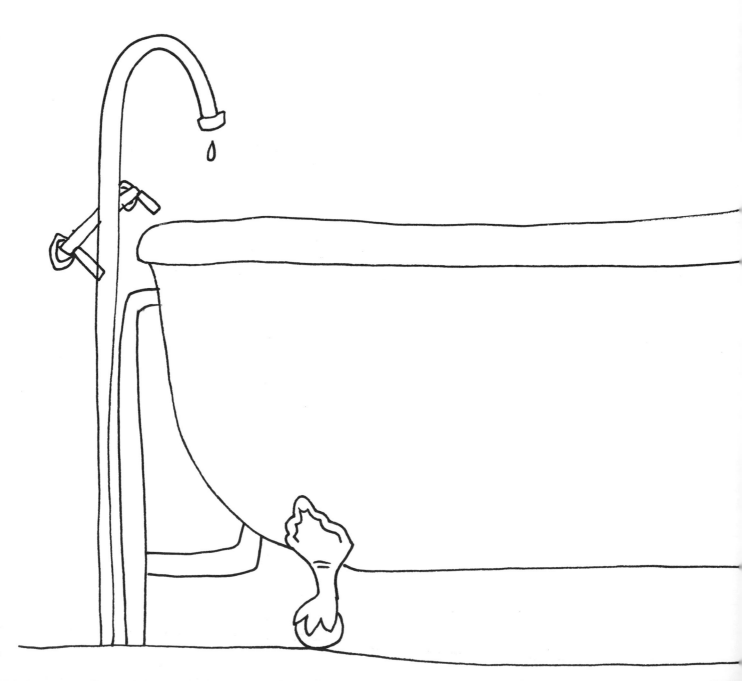

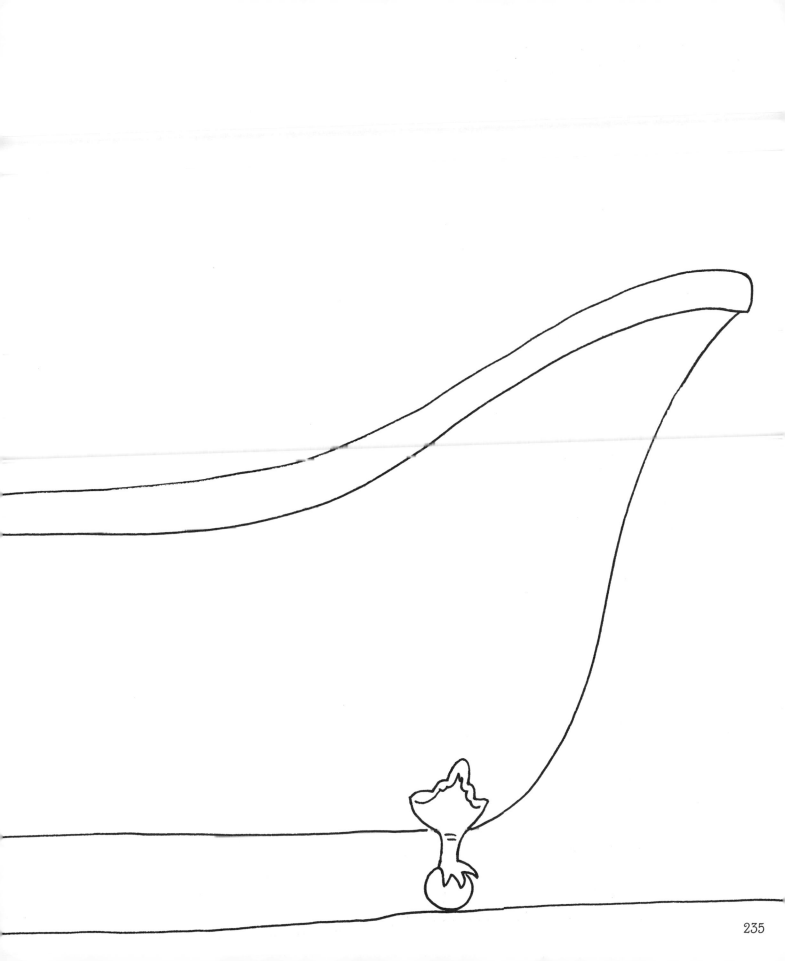

Attention! Attention!

It is your job to count all the elephants!
(The answer is on page 252.)

Draw these Fairies

Most people think they know what fairies look like. We've got the tooth fairy legend as the model, right? Well, maybe other kinds of fairies look different. How would you draw these fairies?

The broken bone fairy. This fairy visits you at night and makes your arm itch under your cast.

The bloody nose fairy. *Usually visits during a test at school.*

The insomnia fairy always visits late at night. You can't see her but she just won't let you get any sleep!

The homework
fairy hides your
assignments in
the books you
left in your
locker.

The daydream fairy
creates fanciful visions
outside the window
during math class.

The puppy love
fairy leads stray,
cuddly, animals to
your door.

What's Your Sign?

If you know the answer to this question, then you know something about astrology: the study of how the movements and placements of stars and planets affect people's lives and personalities. The signs of the zodiac are derived from 12 constellations, or groups of stars, that rise and set in the sky at predictable times of the year. People who buy into astrology think that being born "under" a certain sign gives people that sign's personality traits.

So, how accurate are these signs, anyway? Look over the descriptions and make some guesses. Which description sounds most like you? Which ones sound like your best friend or your brother or sister? After reading each description, write the names of two or more people who sound like they fit that description. Then, turn to the zodiac page on page 252 and see if the birth dates correspond to the guesses you made.

1 People born under this sign tend to be stubborn and hardheaded. However, they also are able to stick with projects long after others give up. They are very dependable, but can be possessive of friends, and may dislike change. They seek pleasure and usually enjoy having nice things. They also enjoy being outside, have good senses of humor, and love to entertain.

_____

_____

2 People born under this sign adapt well to change and seem to be at home wherever they are. They want to know everyone and go everywhere and love adventure. They often know a lot about a lot of things, but don't care to talk about their feelings. They tend to enjoy life to the fullest, are great storytellers, and can be risk-takers. They also love to talk, and can find humor in dark times.

_____

3 People born under this sign love to have an audience. They are creative and often have big ideas. They can be very dramatic and tend to exaggerate. They are enthusiastic and love to have fun, but they can also tire easily of routine and things that they "have" to do. They can be very forgiving and do not hold grudges. When their feelings are hurt, they hide it well.

_____

_____

4 People born under this sign are often very interested in how things work and what makes people tick. They are friendly and happy, but also like to control situations and people. They are often very secretive, yet very emotional. They can be moody and can hold a grudge, and they have excellent memories. They can be very competitive and often enjoy sports.

_____

_____

5 People born under this sign may think of themselves as the center of everything. These people can take charge when they need to get things done. They are very enthusiastic and often act first and think later. They are good friends to others, but can get into silly arguments. They love sports and competitions, and are often good at working with their hands.

_____

_____

6 People born under this sign are often in charge because they like rules and responsibility. It can be hard for them to apologize or to ask for help, and they make careful plans to achieve their goals so they don't have to ask for help. They may only see things as right or wrong, with nothing in between. They think about things before they jump in with both feet. They are very patient.

_____

_____

7 People born under this sign may be very sensitive, and can be very happy or very sad. They can be friends with many different types of people because they understand how people feel. They have big imaginations. They may be very shy, and may tease and joke with others to avoid being the center of attention. They need time by themselves, and love to be near the water.

_____

_____

8 People born under this sign love to gather information and are interested in almost everything. This can make them great students, but it can also make them gossipy. They are good at imitating people and are talkative and funny. They are constantly busy with friends and doing fun things. They are good at giving advice, but don't want to hear too many details.

_____

_____

9 People born under this sign are always looking for the truth. They usually deal fairly with other people and try hard to avoid getting into arguments, but they can get angry when provoked. They treat people as they are treated, have good manners and are often the center of the group, They may shy away from hard work. They usually do not like large crowds.

_____

_____

10 People born under this sign feel that family is very important. Rather than make demands, they often try to be nice to people to get them to do what they want. They can get their feelings hurt easily and may pout instead of talking about it. They make very loyal friends and can usually be trusted. They have excellent memories. They also tend to collect things.

_____

_____

11 People born under this sign like to make things better and often look for ways to help people. Sometimes they expect too much. They often love books and writing, and can be very shy. They are usually very organized and like to know all of the answers. They are very interested in staying in shape and often try to exercise, though they may not care for playing team sports.

_____

_____

12 People born under this sign are extremely independent and have active minds. They tolerate big changes and unusual people well, and can be very unusual themselves. They respect people who work as hard as they do. They like to make people laugh. They are very interested in the past and the future, and may need to be reminded to enjoy the present.

_____

_____

Idiom Quiz

An idiom is a phrase or expression that means something different from what the words actually say. Can you guess these idioms? See page 252 for answers.

Try drawing these idioms:

Out of the frying pan, into the fire.
Looking a gift horse in the mouth.
It's raining cats and dogs.
Hits the spot.
Running around with his head cut off.
Sets the world on fire.
Dumb as a doorknob.
Jump on the bandwagon.
A horse of a different color.

Tune in Next Time!

Before people had computers, TVs, MP3 players, and video games, they had . . . a lot of time on their hands. Now, instead of radio shows, most people listen to podcasts. People make podcasts on all sorts of subjects. There are comedy shows, cooking shows, shows about politics, spaceships, and collecting toys. All of these can be downloaded and listened to on a computer or MP3 player. You can use some stuff lying around your house to make a great podcast. So don't touch that dial, and get started!

First, you are going to need a script. That's where you write down the characters and everything they are going to say. You can finish the script below or write your own.

Find a way to record your podcast. You can use a computer with a microphone (get help from a grown-up if you need it), a video camera (you can always just listen to it), or even an old-fashioned tape recorder. Or, you can do the show for a live audience.

THE 3-INCH SNOW [Intro music]

FALCON: Robin, I have to get to the grocery store! It's snowing like crazy and we only have two loaves of bread and three gallons of milk. [laugh track]
ROBIN: [sound of drinking milk] Make that two gallons.
JAY: [sound of bread being pulled out of a bag and eaten] And one loaf! [laugh track]
FALCON: I'm on my way to find food! [grabs keys and runs out the door] [Sound of running through the snow]
FALCON: There's too much snow to drive my car, but we can't run out of food! This is a job for [superhero music] someone with four-wheel drive!

Before you record, you should practice reading the script using different voices for each character. For the script on the previous page, you could do a deep, loud voice for Falcon, a high, squeaky voice for Robin, and a voice with your mouth full for Jay, since he's eating bread. Some other things you can do are cover your mouth with your hand, talk with an accent, clench your teeth, or even whisper, as long as your audience can understand you. Or, you can always ask your friends to read the different parts.

See the words in [brackets in the script]? These are sound effects. They make a good podcast great. If your script has a horse in it, you can make your audience imagine the horse by tapping blocks on the table. If it's raining, turn on the faucet to make them hear the rain. Use stuff lying around your house. Check out the list below for some ideas, or just walk around and shake stuff to see what it sounds like.

Fire: crumple paper
Walking: Tap shoes heel to toe on different surfaces.
Walking in gravel: Walk shoes in clean cat litter.
Walking in snow: Squeeze a box of cornstarch.
Whoopie cushion: Let a balloon deflate quickly.
Thunder: Shake a sheet of metal.
Rain or a stream: Pour water onto a washcloth.
Rain on a roof: Shake pebbles in a shoebox.
Rushing river or waterfall: Record the white noise from a TV channel that has no station.
Scratching (like a dog): Rub two sheets of sandpaper together.
A baseball hitting a bat: Hit the handles of two wooden spoons together.
Laugh track: On a different recording device, tape a few friends laughing continuously. Each time you need the laugh track, just press the button.

Don't forget about the things in your house that are supposed to make noise, like doorbells, musical instruments, bells, and whistles. And, don't forget to sample your favorite music. If you need help, ask a friend to follow the script and make the sound effects while you do the voices.

So now you have a script, voices, sound effects, and a way to record. Time to record the show and play it for anyone who will listen. Be sure to tell them to vote for you on Podcast Alley. Who knows, you may have enough fans to do another episode!

Answer Key

Take Nine (page 10)

Eat Dirt: Earthworm
Has armor: Armadillo
Drinks out of (butter)cups: Butterfly
Inky feathered friend: Blackbird
Fire-breathing insect?: Dragonfly
NOT on a peanut butter sandwich: Jellyfish
Needs a hundred shoes: Centipede
Don't touch this guy: Porcupine
Hawaiian treat: Pineapple
Meat and bread: Hamburger
Favorite chip: Chocolate
Long, skinny food: Spaghetti
This nut makes green ice cream: Pistachio
This food grows in spears: Asparagus

Fact or Fiction? (page 24)

1. **False.** This rumor was started in the mid-1970s after soft bubble gum first came out. Apparently, some children in or around New York started the rumor, and sales fell in that area until the manufacturer stated that there were no spider eggs in the gum.

2. **True.** A 73-year-old man named Carl Atwood appeared on a local television show to play a game with scratch-off lottery tickets. He came away from the game with over $50,000. As he was crossing the street later in the afternoon, he was struck by a pick-up truck whose driver didn't see him crossing the street.

3. **True.** Although many dream about winning numbers, this woman was so certain she would win that she bought two tickets with the same number. She hit the $24 million jackpot.

4. **False.** This rumor is so widespread because a famous advice columnist published it several years ago. The fact is, birds eat rice all the time from rice fields and seem to do just fine.

5. **True.** The Stanley Cup travels around with the winning hockey team. To protect the Cup, a representative of the NHL now travels with it as it makes its rounds.

6. **False.** This is completely made-up.

7. **False.** No proof has been found, although students of the college usually attributed with producing the prankster are known for their ingenious practical jokes.

8. **True.** Mr. Merhan Karimi Nasseri flew through Paris hoping to make it to England to find distant family there. He left his country without a passport and wasn't allowed to leave the airport in Paris. Since then he has been granted resident status in France and could travel anywhere in Europe if he wanted, but he has decided to remain at the airport.

9. **False.** This made-up legend is simply not true.

10. **False.** Cola is acidic, but does not contain nearly enough acid to dissolve teeth in a short time, if ever.

11. **True.** From about 1934 to 1939, the word "dord" was accidentally listed to mean "density." In fact, there is no word such as "dord" and the word was misread from an editor's note that included the phrase "D or d" as an abbreviation for the word "density."

12. **True.** Thanks to being completely full and also to unseasonable warm January weather, a vat of molasses burst and dumped 2,320,000 gallons of the sweet, sticky concoction through one end of the city. Some people claim that on hot days, you can still smell the molasses!

13. **True,** but it's a trick question. The thought is that since the Earth is coming out of the cold, dark winter into warmer spring, and the hours of day and night are equal, there is something special about this day that allows eggs to be balanced on their ends. The fact is that with a steady hand and the right egg, you can do this any day of the year.

14. **True.** The ingredients listed as cochineal and carmine are made from the ground bodies of bright red beetles that live in Central and South America. The dye is also used in things like shampoo and other products.

15. **False.** While the Coriolis force does make hurricanes turn counterclockwise in the northern hemisphere and clockwise in the southern hemisphere, it is the way the drain and the faucet are shaped and arranged that decides the directions in which water flows.

16. False. This rumor made the rounds on the Internet in the form of an ad for this fake company.

17. True. The seagull walks into the store, grabs one bag of chips at a time, and takes them outside where other gulls gather, rip open the bag, and have a snack.

Put It in Writing (page 28)
1. a) Very small writing means you can concentrate hard, notice small details and may be very smart.
b) Medium writing is about average—more people write this size than any other.
c) Large writing means you are fun to talk to and enthusiastic. If your writing is very large, it can mean you get excited or angry easily, and you like looking at the big picture.

2. a) Writing that stays on a straight line is the way most people write.
b) Writing that runs "uphill" means you like setting goals and are optimistic.
c) Writing that runs "uphill" a lot may mean you are very happy, and maybe a little hyper.
d) Writing that runs "downhill" means that you might be a little sad on the day of the writing
e) Writing that runs "downhill" a lot may mean you are going through a hard time.

3. a) Writing that stays on the line is how most people write. It means people can depend on you.
b) Writing that moves up and down means you can be a little careless and have a tendency to be late, but you may have many talents.

4. a) Writing that slants straight up and down may mean you are sincere and don't get upset too easily.
b) Writing that slants to the right a little is how most people write.
c) Writing that slants to the right a lot means you are spontaneous and affectionate. If your writing slants far to the right, it can mean you are nervous and very sensitive.
d) Writing that slants to the left a little means you think with your head and not your heart.
e) Writing that slants to the left a lot can mean you hide your feelings.
*Note that some people who are left-handed have handwriting that slants to the left. In that case, use the descriptions for slanting to the right.

5. a) Writing lines that are very close together mean you don't care about expensive things, and it may mean you get confused easily.
b) Writing lines with more space between them are the average kind of writing.
c) Writing lines that are very far apart mean you are a very clear thinker.

6. a) Letters that are always connected mean you are good at reasoning.
b) Letters that are sometimes connected shows sometimes you think with your head and sometimes with your heart.
c) Letters that are not connected may mean you jump to conclusions. It can also mean that you learned to use the computer for most of your writing and don't write very often.

7. a) Lowercase letters that are all the same size mean you try to do the right thing.
b) Lowercase letters that are different sizes mean that you can change your mind easily.

8. a) If your lowercase letter o is always closed at the top, it means you keep secrets.
b) If your lowercase letter o is always open at the top, it means you say what you think.
c) If your lowercase letter o sometimes open, it means you mean what you say.
d) If your lowercase letter o knotted at the top with a loop, it means you are very private.

9. a) If the cross on your lowercase t is short, it means you pay close attention to things, but maybe tend to sit back and watch instead of jump in and do.
b) If the cross on your lowercase t is long, it means you love life.
c) If the cross on your lowercase t is high you are creative and imaginative.
d) If the cross on your lowercase t is low you care for others.
e) If the cross on your lowercase t is thick you are stubborn and it may mean you have a bad temper.
f) If the cross on your lowercase t is thin it means you take time to do things right.
g) If the cross on your lowercase t is starting thin and getting thick, it means you take a long time to get angry.
h) If the cross on your lowercase t is starting thick and getting thin, it means you get angry quickly and get over it quickly.

i) If the cross on your lowercase t is slanting up, you reach your goals.

j) If the cross on your lowercase t is slanting down, you have strong ideas and you like to have things your way.

10. a) If your f, g, p, q, and y loops are very long, you probably play sports or lift weights.

b) If your f, g, p, q, and y loops are very short, you probably aren't very strong.

c) If your f, g, p, q, and y loops are very wide, you like to tell tall tales.

d) If your f, g, p, q, and y loops are looped in knots, you keep secrets.

e) If your f, g, p, q, and y loops are not looped but come back up to the right, you were in a big hurry when you write this, and maybe all the time.

11. a) If your uppercase letters B, D, and G are wider at the top, people can fool you easily.

b) If your uppercase letters B, D, and G are wider at the bottom, you don't believe everything you hear.

12. a) If your uppercase letters are like printed letters, you are good at building things or at doing things with your hands.

b) If your uppercase letters are like your lowercase letters, except bigger, you aren't trendy.

c) If your uppercase letters are big and rough, with lots of swirls, you may like to show off.

13. a) If the dots over your lowercase letter i are low, you think about things and do them carefully.

b) If the dots over your lowercase letter i are high, you like to find things out. You may be nosy.

c) If the dots over your lowercase letter i are to the left, you tend to wait until the last minute.

d) If the dots over your lowercase letter i are to the right, you may do something first and think about it later.

e) If the dots over your lowercase letter i are heavy and dark, you like owning nice things.

f) If the dots over your lowercase letter i are light, other people can talk you into things.

g) If the dots over your lowercase letter i are shaped like a circle or a heart or any other unusual shape, you like to follow the latest trends.

h) If the dots over your lowercase letter i are missing, you may be forgetful and disorganized.

14. a) If your letters with top loops (b, d, f, h, k, l) are low, you may not pretend a lot.

b) If your letters with top loops (b, d, f, h, k, l) are high, you love to imagine how things could turn out.

c) If your letters with top loops (b, d, f, h, k, l) are wide, you like to hear nice things about yourself, and you believe what you hear.

d) If your letters with top loops (b, d, f, h, k, l) are made with lines instead of loops, you are an unusual person, and have your own opinions.

e) If your letters with top loops (b, d, f, h, k, l) are printed, you might be artistic.

f) If your letters with top loops (b, d, f, h, k, l) are tied in a knot, you are very private.

Proverb Completion (page 32)

Laughter is the best medicine.
A bird in the hand is worth two in the bush.
Don't count your chickens before they hatch.
No news is good news.
Don't look a gift horse in the mouth.
What goes around comes around.
Every cloud has a silver lining.
The more things change, the more they stay the same.
The early bird catches the worm.
Good fences make good neighbors.
Measure twice, cut once.
When life gives you lemons, make lemonade.
If at first you don't succeed, try, try again.
Actions speak louder than words.
If you can't beat 'em, join 'em.
You can't judge a book by its cover.
Birds of a feather flock together.

The Next Text Thing (page 36)

SUP = What's Up?
GB = Goodbye
NE1 = Anyone
BBIAM = Be Back In A Minute
UGTBK = You've Got To Be Kidding
WAN2TLK = Want To Talk?
THNX = Thanks
L8RG8R = Later, Gator
AWC = After while, crocodile
HRU = How Are You?
G2G = Got To Go
CUL8R = See You Later
CIAO = Goodbye (Italian)

BFF = Best Friend Forever
.02 = Your Two Cents (your opinion)
K = OK
?4U = Question For You
BCOS = Because
HAND = Have a nice day
BHL8 = Be Home Late
EZY = Easy
IDK = I Don't Know
IMHO = In My Humble Opinion
JK = Just Kidding
IG2R = I've Got To Run
KEYA = "Key" (talk to) You Later—like "See Ya!"
PU = That stinks!
ROFL = Rolling on the Floor Laughing
GR8 = Great
IC = I See (I understand)
BIBI = Bye-bye

What's Not to Like? (page 50)

1–10 points: Aww, you're really sweet. You care about others and about animals. Be sure to take care of yourself and be your own best friend, too!

11–20 points: You have a big brain! Your friends probably look to you for smart answers. While you're being smart, don't forget to let your hair down and have fun, too.

21–30 points: Bwah hah hah! You are funny and love to make people laugh. Remember that people will like seeing your serious side, too.

31–40 points: You get the best-all-around award. People trust you to say and do the right thing. Remember that nobody's perfect, so cut yourself some slack sometimes!

41–50 points: You are the greeter at the door. You are outgoing and friendly. Sometimes, though, it's fun to sit back and watch the party rather than run it.

51–60 points: You reach your goals! You make sure that you accomplish what you set out to do. Be nice to those who help you out, and don't forget to be happy when your friends do well, too.

Beghilosz (page 59)

Today was going to be a BIG day. I was in a hurry to go to a carnival after school but had a map test to study for first. I had left my social studies book at home, so I got my GLOBE out of my closet, and looked up the places I needed to know for my map test, like OHIO. Then, my phone rang. It was my friend LESLIE. She was finished with homework and wanted to go to the carnival and BOB for apples, for some reason. I said sure and met her outside. We ran into our friend BILL and all went together. First, we went to the EGG toss. I shattered both of my EGGS but my friends did pretty well. We stopped by the petting zoo where they had some GEESE, some BEES, some EELS, and some HOGS. We went on some crazy rides. On a roller coaster called the Crazy SLEIGH, I got so dizzy all I could do was HOBBLE away and try not to LOSE my lunch. I was afraid my brain would OOZE out of my ears. We were hungry and could hear the SIZZLE of fries, but my friends wanted LOLLIES. Finally, we found the place where LESLIE could BOB for apples and win a prize. She put on a BIB and some GOGGLES and watched as they used a HOSE to refill the barrel. Then she stuck her head under water, opened her mouth, and tried to GOBBLE an apple. Soon, she lifted her head and shouted with GLEE. She got an apple! She went to get her prize. The man running the game said, "You are not ELIGIBLE to win because you have to be under age 5, but we'll make an exception. You have your choice of a blow-up IGLOO or a set of doll SHOES. LESLIE laughed and took the IGLOO for her little brother. We left to look for some food to fill our BELLIES.

Kitchen Impossible (page 68)

1. Egg poacher
2. Pasta fork
3. Lid opener
4. Hand-crank pasta machine
5. Corn scraper
6. Crank-turn apple peeler
7. Pickle fork
8. Food mill
9. Old-fashioned juicer

Senri-me, Senryu (page 72)

1. Oh wait, she just has two.
2. They're fortified with iron.
3. Five-second rule. Yum.
4. Who has the stomach flu.
5. Except for leprechauns.
6. Of Mom's old minivan.

All for One (Meaning (page 78)

2. religious leaders
3. shoes
4. food
5. paper money
6. amazed or surprised
7. happy
8. child
9. friend
10. party
11. argument
12. flustered or confused
13. angry
14. problem
15. pants

Brainbenders (page 83)

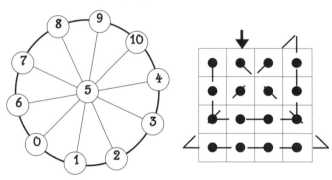

Eyewitness Questions (page 84)

1. 4
2. Man holding mannequin
3. One Way sign
4. Peace sign
5. Goat
6. Bikini
7. 1
8. two kissing; one sitting there
9. mailbox
10. 5 (don't forget the one in the car)
11. 3
12. yes
13. a cup with a straw
14. 14
15. Answers will vary

Something in Common (page 111)

2. Each word begins with the last letter of the word before it. So the next word would be any beginning with the letter y.
3. Add the letter r to each word to make a new word: stream, drip, scrape, pretty, marker, part, strand, crops, sport, crane, diver, shore. The next word should become a new word when you add the letter "r," such as potion = portion.
4. Each letter begins with the first letter of each planet in the solar system. (Yes, we included Pluto, but it's not really a planet.)
5. Each word, added to the word after it, makes a new word. The next word could be "out."
6 Each word begins with the first letter of the numbers 1–10. The next word should start with the letter "e" for "eleven."
7. Each word becomes a new word if you remove the first and last letters: loud, lower, cow, ear, ate, pin, rink, at, or, one, pen, and owe, in the sample word. There are endless possibilities!
8. Each word begins with a letter that begins each day of the week.
9. OK, sure, these are all foods, but they are also words that begin with the letter of each color in the spectrum. Think ROY G BIV.
10. Hey, we got tired. It's alphabetical order, plain and simple. Add your own j-word here.

Number Numbers (page 180)

29 Days in February in a Leap Year
8 Planets in our Solar System
5,280 Feet in a Mile
88 Keys in a Piano
9 Players on a Baseball Field
3 Blind Mice, See How They Run
7 Days in a Week
52 Cards in a Deck
26 Letters in the Alphabet
12 Months in a Year
18 Holes on a Golf Course
206 Bones in the Body
12 Eggs in a Dozen
1000 Words that a Picture is Worth
64 Squares on a Chessboard

The Code to Rome (Page 190)

Q. How many months have 28 days?
A. I XII XII   XV VI   XX VIII V XIII
   All   of   them.

Q. How many birds can you fit into an empty nest?
A. One. After that, it isn't empty anymore.

Q. How do you make a slow horse fast?
A. Stop feeding it!

Q. What did the lawyer name his daughter?
A. Sue!

1. C
2. B
3. A
4. C
5. VII, XIX, XX, XXIV, XXV, XXVII, XXVIII, XXX, XXXI, XXXIV
6. XL, L, LV, LIX, LXI, LXII, LXIV, LXV, LXX, LXXIX
7. XC, XCV, XCVIII, CI, CXL, CL, CLXIV, CCL, CCXC, CCC
8. DXCVII
9. MCDXXXVII
10. MMMCMXLIX

Spot the Differences (page 204)

Wizard Keys (page 198)

Cliches. OK? (page 218)

Blind as a bat.
Strong as an ox.
Snug as a bug in a rug.
Sly like a fox.

Proud as a peacock.
Clear as a bell.
Hard as a rock.
Deep as a well.

Dead as a doornail.
Sharp as a tack.
Thin as a rail.
Dark as night.

White as a sheet.
White as snow.
Busy as a bee.
Straight as an arrow.

Light as air.
Quiet as a mouse.
Soft as a baby's bottom.
Big as a house.

Sick as a dog.
Flat as a pancake.
Happy as a clam.

Attention! Attention! (page 236)

102 elephants

What's Your Sign (page 240)

1. Taurus (March 21–April 20)
2. Sagittarius (November 23–December 22)
3. Leo (July 23–August 21)
4. Scorpio (October 24–November 22)
5. Aries (March 21–April 21)
6. Capricorn (December 23–January 20)
7. Pisces (February 20–March 20)
8. Gemini (May 22–June 21)
9. Libra (September 24–October 23)
10. Cancer (June 22–July 22)
11. Virgo (August 22–September 23)
12. Aquarius (January 21–February 19)

Triangle (page 219)

```
        A
      B   C
    D   E   F
  G   H   I   J
K   L   M   N   O
```

One way of winning the game is to leave the top hole (A) open.
1. Jump F over C to A. Remove C.
2. Jump D over E to F. Remove E.
3. Jump A over B to D. Remove B.
4. Jump G over D to B. Remove D.
5. Jump J over F to C. Remove F.
6. Jump M over I to F. Remove I.
7. Jump F over C to A. Remove C.
8. Jump A over B to D. Remove B.
9. Jump O over N to M. Remove N.
10. Jump L over M to N. Remove M.
11. Jump D over H to M. Remove H.
12. Jump N over M to L. Remove N.
13. Jump K over L to M. Remove L.
The peg on space M will be the last peg.

Idiom Quiz (page 242)

He's a lame duck president.
She can really shovel in the food!
Junior is on top of the world.
He always bends over backwards for friends.
Mom's sure bent out of shape!
Dad always starts the day with a cup of Joe.

As you can see, your blank pages start here.